COPENHAGEN OPERA HOUSE

Richard Brett
John Offord

**ENTERTAINMENT
TECHNOLOGY PRESS**

Buildings & Projects Series

front cover photograph: Thomas Nørdam Andersen

COPENHAGEN OPERA HOUSE

Richard Brett, John Offord

Entertainment Technology Press

Copenhagen Opera House

© Richard Brett, John Offord and contributors

First edition published June 2006
by Entertainment Technology Press Ltd
The Studio, High Green, Great Shelford, Cambridge CB2 5EG
Internet: www.etnow.com

ISBN 1 904031 42 0

A title within the
Entertainment Technology Press Buildings & Projects Series
Series editor: John Offord

All rights reserved. No part of this publication may be reproduced in any material form (including photocopying or storing in any medium by electronic means and whether or not transiently or incidentally to some other use of this publication) without the written permission of the copyright holder except in accordance with the provisions of the Copyright, Designs and Patents Act 1988. Applications for the copyright holder's written permission to reproduce any part of this publication should be addressed to the publishers.

CODE / COH03 - 1006

CONTENTS

1 INTRODUCTION 9
2 THE ROYAL DANISH OPERA 13
3 THE BIRTH OF OPERAEN 17
4 THE ROLE OF THE THEATRE CONSULTANT 29
5 THE DEVELOPMENT OF THE AUDITORIUM 37
   Neil Morton, Richard Brett
6 THE STUDIO STAGE 57
   Neil Morton, Richard Brett
7 THE ACOUSTIC DESIGN OF OPERAEN 71
   Jeremy Newton
8 CONSTRUCTION AND EQUIPPING OF OPERAEN 89
   Richard Brett
9 STAGE ENGINEERING IN OPERAEN 109
   Richard Brett, Clive Odom, Dave Ludlam
10 STAGE LIGHTING IN OPERAEN 159
   John Whitaker, Richard Brett
11 LIGHTING CONTROL AND NETWORKING 173
   Ulrich Kunkel
12 ARCHITECTURAL LIGHTING OF OPERAEN 189
   Jonathan Speirs, Keith Bradshaw
13 SOUND TECHNOLOGY IN OPERAEN 203
   Charles Wass, Richard Brett

14 THE ORGAN 221

15 THE VIEWS OF THE USERS 227
   Nikolaj Jensen, Kasper Holte, Frank Andersen

16 TECHNICAL SCHEDULES 233

17 AN IMPRESSION OF OPERAEN 259
   Tobi Tobias

ACKNOWLEDGEMENTS

The production of this book would not have been possible without the expert input of Jeremy Newton of Arup Acoustics, Jonathan Speirs and Keith Bradshaw of Speirs and Major Associates, Neil Morton, John Whitaker, Charles Wass and Dave Ludlam of Theatreplan LLP, Nikolaj Jensen, Ulrich Kunkel, Kasper Holte, Frank Andersen and Per Frendahl who provided information and specialist sections covering their own area of involvement with the Copenhagen Opera House project.

In addition, Søren Nylin, Sten Hassing Møller, Louise Pedersen and Susanne Ørskov of The Royal Danish Theatre helped us in various ways to pull copy and pictures together. We are grateful for permission to use the piece on her observations on the building by Tobi Tobias.

Unless stated otherwise, photographs are by Richard Brett, John Offord, Clive Odom, Rob Harris of Arup Acoustics, Adam Mørk and Lars Schmidt.

To all those mentioned we are extremely grateful, and also to Poul Tønder and Thomas Riishøj of Gobo Lighting of Copenhagen who put the original pressure on us to produce what started as an idea for a potential magazine feature and ended up as a book.

Richard Brett
John Offord

1 INTRODUCTION

This is the story of what is probably the best modern opera house in the world. As our client, Mr Mærsk Mc-Kinney Møller, announced, it was to be 'second to none'. And certainly it has first class acoustics, excellent ambience, very good sightlines, modern and very comprehensive equipment and extensive foyer and back stage facilities. There is a good balance between its design, its quality and its functions. And it was constructed as a gift to the Danish nation. Many theatre groups and organisations around the world will be very envious of the Danish Royal Theatre, the company charged with performing opera and ballet on its spacious main stage and offering everything from master classes to chamber opera on its studio stage.

What makes a good opera house? There will never be total agreement on that question but clearly many specific features are of great importance. The Copenhagen Opera has both style and function; neither the design, the construction nor the equipment has been compromised. Not everyone will like

Copenhagen Operaen from across the harbour. *Photo: Adam Mørk*

the architecture, interior design or backstage planning and theatre technicians will debate the type and functions of the stage machinery and of the lighting and sound installations. But while the users who take over theatre buildings are often plagued with a period in which installations or finishes are still being completed, that was not so in Copenhagen. The building was taken over complete and as seen, and the contractors moved out of the building on that day and away from the site within a month. One of the stage engineering contractors had to complete the setting up of some stage wagon drives and was also asked to remain through to the opening of the first production to be on hand if the crew had any malfunctions or faults that had not been covered in the training periods. The Royal Theatre also had the luxury of more than three months from taking over the building to prepare for their first production – compare that with the opening of the Royal Opera House in London in which the preparation period was the same number of weeks.

This book may have been written in the honeymoon period when everything seems new and exciting but trouble lies ahead. To those involved, it doesn't feel like it. The technical director, Nikolaj Jensen, confessed to finding moving in and using the stages uneventful – everyone was very happy with the installations, everything was going well and he actually had time on his hands. Since then there have been some problems but these should not be unexpected. They have been handled professionally and will help the crew prepare for the longer-term future. Richard Brett and the Theatreplan team, along with a number of the other consultants, have written chapters to explain their contributions to the planning and technical aspects of the opera. But the user's opinions are vital and Nikolaj and others from the Royal Theatre have summarised their views in this book.

Acoustics were to be excellent for all performances in both of the auditoria. The brief given to Arup Acoustics led by Rob Harris was to achieve first class room acoustics and to eliminate all intrusive noise whether from outside or from sources within the building itself. This set Rob on a collision course with many aspects of live theatre; motor noise, luminaire noise, air velocities, even thin sheet steel cladding which found its way onto some of the galleries. Acoustic consultants generally advise other members of the design team and don't actually have a budget for their works. This caused the project manager much grief as, understandably, Arups called for changes and additions to achieve their goals, and this led to Rob becoming known as Rob 'no budget' Harris! That was probably no worse than Richard Brett who had a budget of

£20m (€30m, US$37m) to control and was told by Mr Møller on a number of occasions that he was the most expensive consultant on the project: Mr Møller did acknowledge however that this was a reference to the equipment budget which was higher than he expected, and not to Theatreplan's fee!

This book is therefore a series of chapters by some of those whose skill, experience and hard work got this project completed so successfully in a very short time and by others who have taken over and are using the opera. There were many others who have not been able to contribute to the book but they are all part of the process of completing this building. The book stands as a tribute to all of these people.

Richard Brett

2 THE ROYAL DANISH OPERA

The Royal Danish Opera is part of the Royal Danish Theatre, which is one of the few theatres in the world where opera, ballet, drama and music are staged by the same institution. The Royal Danish opera is the only company in Denmark with a permanent stage, and the organisation's aim is to become the leading Nordic opera, presenting to the world the greatest voices of Scandinavia and celebrating a repertoire of contemporary opera productions focusing on epic storytelling.

In 2000, the A P Møller and Chastine Mc-Kinney Møller Foundation – headed by Denmark's wealthiest man, Mr Mærsk Mc-Kinney Møller – donated an opera house to the Danish people which was to be erected on the Copenhagen waterfront and to be used by the Royal Theatre.

Construction of the new Opera House, at a cost of approximately 335 million

The new Copenhagen Opera House was inaugurated with a royal command performance on 15th January 2005.   *Photo: Lars Schmidt*

euros, was rapid and the house was completed on 1st October 2004, little more than three years after work started on the site.

The new Opera House, or Operaen in Danish, is situated in the heart of Copenhagen and has been designed to facilitate large opera and ballet productions. It also features a studio stage seating up to 200 for the presentation of chamber operas and ballets, experimental works, readings and seminars. The building, designed by leading Danish architect Henning Larsen, was inaugurated with a royal command performance on 15th January 2005.

In 1999, theatre director of the Royal Danish Theatre, Michael Christiansen, appointed the then 26-year-old Kasper Bech Holten as artistic director of the Royal Danish Opera. At the same time, the acclaimed Danish conductor Michael Schønwandt was appointed as music director of the Royal Danish Opera and the Royal Danish Orchestra.

As a working team they have staged new productions of Tchaikovsky's *Pique Dame* and Ligeti's *Le Grand Macabre* at the Royal Danish Theatre, and are currently (2003-2006) the creative team behind a new production of Wagner's *Der Ring des Nibelungen*.

Since 2000 it has been the stated policy of the current theatre opera management to stage at least one Danish premiere or world premiere of a new large-scale contemporary opera production every season. This has already resulted in several world premieres, with more planned for the future – one being *Kafka's Trial* by Poul Rudens, who achieved international acclaim for his *The Handmaid's Tale* in 2000.

The Royal Danish Opera ensemble is celebrated for its accomplished Wagner and Strauss singers, and correspondingly, these repertoires are focal points of the Royal Danish Opera. However, operas by Verdi, Rossini and Puccini, as well as those by lesser-known composers, are also featured.

At the same time, the Opera has engaged in developing a profile within the baroque repertoire, most notably with Andreas Scholl's internationally acclaimed debut as *Giulio Cesare*, accompanied by period instrument ensemble Concerto Copenhagen conducted by the world-famous Danish harpsichordist and conductor Lars Ulrik Mortensen.

The Royal Danish Theatre has embarked on an immense new journey from one to four houses. With the new main house it will be able to stage the Romantic opera repertoire in full scale and benefit from state-of-the-art technology and perfect acoustics.

The old home of the Opera, the Old Stage at the Royal Danish Theatre which dates from 1874, will in future be home to the Royal Danish Ballet. However, the Royal Danish Opera will still perform operas here that require less space, such as baroque and classical operas, just as the Royal Danish Ballet will perform larger ballets in the new Opera House.

In 2008, under the auspices of the Royal Theatre, a new three-stage playhouse will be completed on the Copenhagen waterfront opposite the Opera House. All art forms presented by the Royal Danish Theatre will then enjoy optimal working conditions. In addition, a new central production facility, including workshops and storage space, is planned to be constructed to serve all these production spaces.

*The Opera House from Frederikskirken
Photo Adam Mørk.*

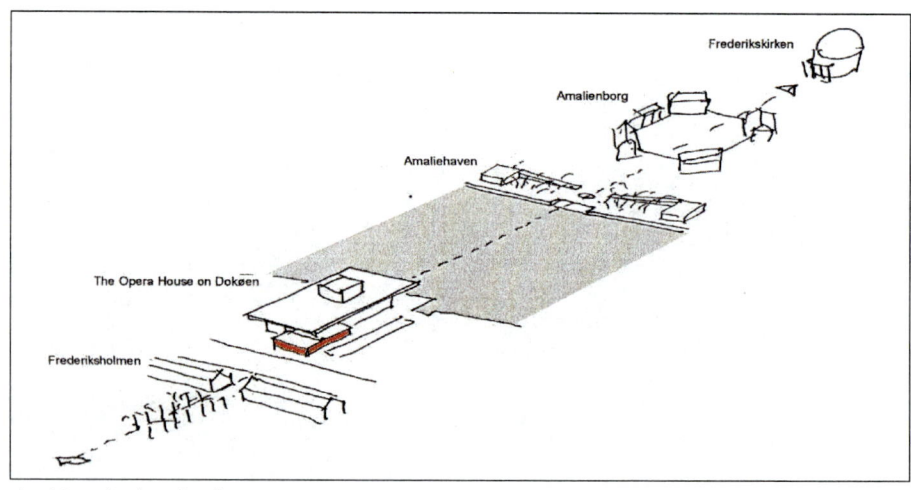

Architect's sketch of city axis.

3 THE BIRTH OF OPERAEN

In 2000 the City of Copenhagen, in cooperation with Copenhagen Harbour, the real estate company Freja, and the Ministry of Environment and Energy, asked three architectural companies – West 8, Sjoerd Soeters, and Henning Larsens Tegnestue – to prepare a volume study of the Copenhagen Harbour in order to define and control the future urban development of the area. Henning Larsens Tegnestue (HLT) was responsible for the inner harbour and the other two companies were responsible for the northern and southern parts of the harbour, respectively.

HLT's vision for the inner harbour was to develop the area by mixing residential and commercial buildings with large public cultural institutions to create a dynamic city life. It was considered by the City that this would create a rich variety in the urban environment, and by adding quality and coherence to the areas, the harbour would provide an attraction for the citizens of Copenhagen as well as visitors from all over the world.

Three large buildings were envisaged, situated at Dokøen, Christiansholm and Kvæsthusbroen, in order to create a new strong cultural centre with the water and the harbour as the unifying elements. Apart from the three public cultural institutions the concept included wide public harbour promenades along the water as well as minor public spaces. Sailing traffic across the harbour between the cultural institutions, supplemented by other activities in the area, would create a unique and dynamic urban quarter for all the Nordic countries.

The building at Dokøen (now the Opera House) was placed on the Amalienborg axis as a counterpart to the Frederikskirken (Frederik's Church) – the two large buildings forming the termination points of the east/west axis from the harbour and across the Amalienborg Square.

The studies prepared by the three architectural companies were presented to the City of Copenhagen and to the public at an exhibition in 2000.

At the same time the AP Møller Foundation expressed a wish to donate a large cultural building to Denmark, an idea that exactly matched the vision for the inner harbour. In 2000 it was therefore decided that the A.P.Møller and Chastine Mc-Kinney Møller Foundation would donate Denmark's

The Amalienborg axis: a view from the Opera House to the Frederikskirken (centre left).　　　　　　　　　　　　　　　　　　　　　　　　　　Photo: Lars Schmidt

View of Operaen from the south-east.　　　　　　　　　　　Photo: Adam Mørk

first separate modern opera and ballet house with a dignified and dramatic siting at the termination point of the historical Amalienborg axis and that Henning Larsens Tegnestue was appointed architect for the project.

Opera at Dokøen

The inspired location of the Opera, standing on a 41,000sq.m site, is one of the best positions within the Copenhagen Harbour. Placed on the axis from the Frederikskirken and Amalienborg, it is also visible from the entire inner harbour from Knippelsbro to Kastellet.

The Opera was planned to be filled with activities from early morning till late at night all the year round, and, together with the other cultural institutions at Holmen, will contribute to an active and inspirational urban space. The design of the Opera allows the audience in the foyer to view the harbour to the west, with the grand arrival plaza facing the old Frederiksstaden (Frederik's Town) across the water. Oriented towards the western evening sky, the covered arrival plaza welcomes the audience approaching by boat or from the wide harbour promenade at Dokøen. To the east, the strict symmetry of the building is broken by the studio stage – Takkelloftet – which meets the offset axis of Holmen in Philip de Langes Allé.

The concept of the arrival plaza gives the city a new covered space without columns and provides for a multiplicity of functions. The Royal Theatre also now has an option of performing on a floating stage in the harbour with the audience placed on the plaza under the cantilevered roof. The opera guests arrive and depart from the plaza, which is also used during intervals. In addition, a café facing southwest provides an experience not only of the Opera, but also the harbour and a wide view of the city.

The space between the cantilevered roof and the granite surfaced plaza is projected into the harbour with a 180 degree panoramic view along the harbour from Knippelsbro and over the city centre with its towers and spires to the northern harbour entrance towards the Sound.

The importance of the Opera is accentuated by its location on a separate island, as new canals have been established on both sides of the building.

However, the Opera House is not intended to stand alone on Dokøen, as the original plans included blocks of apartments to the north and south when the new quarter is completed. These residential buildings were planned to form a quiet and discreet background for the Opera, which will be the landmark on the waterfront as well as towards Takkelloftsgraven where it ends at Philip de Langes Allé in the centre of the space between the two bridges. Across the canal two fine, old, historically preserved warehouses close the canal space, which is accentuated by trimmed trees on Dokøen similar to those on Christianshavns Canal.

The backstage area of the Opera is designed as a low and massive block forming part of the cadence of the future residential buildings, whereas the front of the house is visually integrated in the harbour space with the auditorium floating in the light and bright foyer.

The future residential buildings on Dokøen may also 'float' above an open ground floor with cafés and shops alternating with openings to lively inner courtyards.

Structure of the Opera

To the west the Opera is sited towards the harbour and the Frederiksstaden and to the east towards Holmen. The Opera respects the differences in scale as the floating roof to the west relates to the larger scale, ie the harbour and the Frederiksstaden, whereas the low, more substantial block to the east relates to a smaller scale, characteristic of Holmen.

The auditorium shell viewed through the foyer facade.   Photo: Adam Mørk

HLT views Dokøen as an urban harbour island providing a different visitor experience to the adjacent Frederiksholm, which appears more like a 'green garden' with small houses and old chestnut trees. An opera house comprises a variety of functions and rooms and is divided into two main areas: front of house and backstage. Front of house consists of the foyer and the auditorium, whereas backstage holds the stage area including workshop facilities, dressing rooms, costume shops, administration offices and rehearsal facilities for singers, choir, soloists, orchestra and ballet.

The spectacular 'floating' cantilevered roof is the unifying element of the Opera House, and its architectural function is to bring together and control all the various elements. The interaction of the auditorium shell and the public harbour space is considered to be the key element of the design. From a distance you can see the golden maple-panelled auditorium shell through the foyer facade – whereas the fly tower indicates the position of the stage. The foyer and the auditorium float between the arrival level and the huge roof, increasing the scale towards the harbour.

Front of House

In the daytime the plaza will function as a vital pedestrian centre of the harbour as a result of the activities at the Opera. Guests will be using the restaurant facilities and the café, and events will be taking place in the foyer and in the auditoria. In the evening, the character of the plaza changes as the light from the foyer radiates over the area where cars drop off audience for the opera.

The foyer encircles the prominent form of the auditorium, which – inspired by a conch – floats between the floor and the cantilevered roof. The foyer floor leads you through the shell to the auditorium stalls area, and visual links through the opening between the foyer and the auditorium draw you to the heart of the conch.

From the arrival level the audience is led by two wide staircases to the main balcony on the first floor, where two further staircases lead to the upper balconies and to a banquet area which holds 200 guests on the fourth floor. Two long bars with leather fronts serve the audience on the first two levels, whereas two smaller bars serve the upper balconies. The arrival level and the main balcony are furnished with leather furniture. Radial bridges connect the balconies of the foyer with the shell, thus creating a parallel to the 'see and be seen' experience in the auditorium, as you can overlook the people-filled foyer from the balconies. Turn around and you are provided with a scenographic view over the harbour, with the Copenhagen skyline against the evening sky.

Lifts and cloakrooms are placed on each foyer level on both sides of the auditorium, and stairs from the ground floor in the northern part of the foyer lead down to the cloakrooms in the basement.

The Conch

The form of the auditorium is inspired by the magic of a conch: round and smooth, it embraces a world of fantasy and mystery, the roar of the sea conjuring up images of a musical instrument. And this image obtains tangibility through the choice of the material used: stained, lacquered maple – inspired by a violin.

The auditorium, with its classical form with parterre and horseshoe balconies (three for the audience and a technical gallery above) creates an intense vertical room surrounded by an audience which makes the 'see and be seen' experience a part of the opera magic. The intimate room with steps and unbroken, mildy curved rows of seats, accentuates the meeting between art and audience. The auditorium holds from about 1,470 to 1,650 guests depending on the size of the flexible orchestra pit.

The golden maple panels on the exterior of the shell continue through the big central opening to the auditorium where they end in the balconies. The walls are dark stained solid maple elements, and the floor is smoked oak. Horizontal recesses in various lengths and depths on all walls including box walls and balcony fronts are not just for decoration; their function is to give the perfect acoustic ambience. The seats are covered with velour in accordance with the Royal Theatre tradition.

A wealth of star-like spots inserted in the gold-leaf covered ceiling lights up the auditorium. The balcony fronts have integrated lights in the horizontal recesses as a decoration, and some more small spots are placed in the balcony soffits to give light to the balcony seats.

Open balconies with raised podiums on the sides have replaced the classical boxes in order to ensure optimum acoustics and sightlines. On the third balcony standing places take advantage of the good sightlines to the stage.

Studio Stage

The studio stage (or Takkelloftet, the 'rigging loft') has a separate entrance from Takkelloftsgraven. The foyer, oriented towards Holmen, makes the studio stage an independent entity, but at the same time it forms part of the other stage facilities. The studio stage foyer affords a view to the north towards the harbour, to the east towards Philip de Langes Allé, and to the south along Takkelloftsgraven towards the spire of Vor Frelsers Kirke (Our Saviour's Church) in Christianshavn.

The studio stage is a totally flexible black box, which provides around 200 seats, partly on a retractable podium, and on 13 mobile towers that move on air cushions allowing a large number of configurations.

Orchestra Rehearsal Room

The orchestra rehearsal room is one of the biggest rehearsal rooms of the Opera, holding 120 performers, including soloists and choir. The box-in-box structured room is placed 14m below sea level under the auditorium and close to the orchestra pit, which facilitates the easy transportation of musical instruments. The lighting design of the room consists of a white artificial daylight along the walls and a warmer indoor working light in the ceiling.

The form of the auditorium is inspired by the magic of a conch. Pictured above is the golden maple panelled exterior shell.   Photo: Adam Mørk.

Backstage

Staff and performers enter through the stage door in the east façade. From the manned reception area there is access to the dressing rooms, costume shops, and the administration offices, all located around the stage area and connected by open corridors over five-storeys with skylights, which provide a soft light on the white concrete walls all the way down to the ground floor.

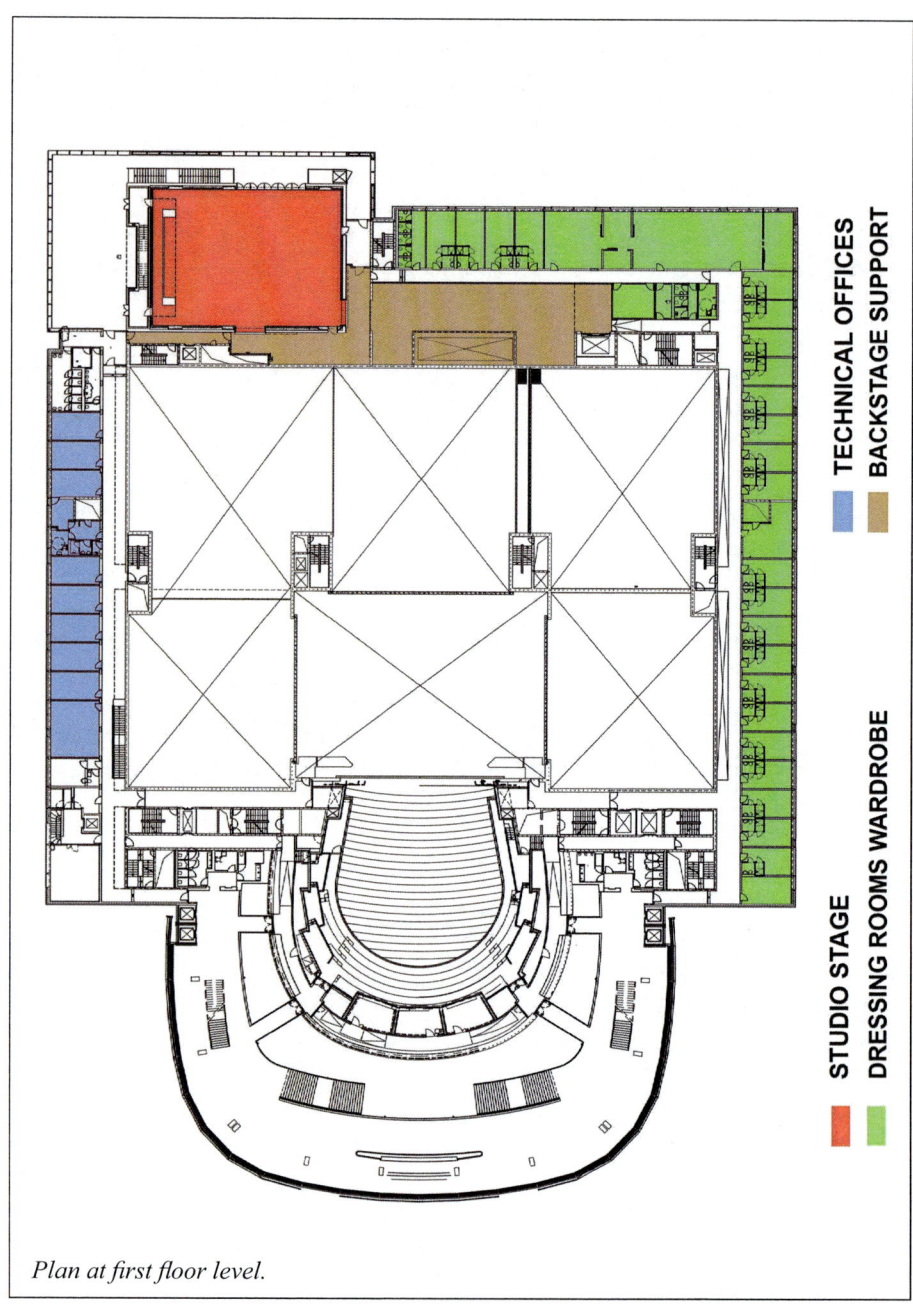

Plan at first floor level.

24 Copenhagen Opera House

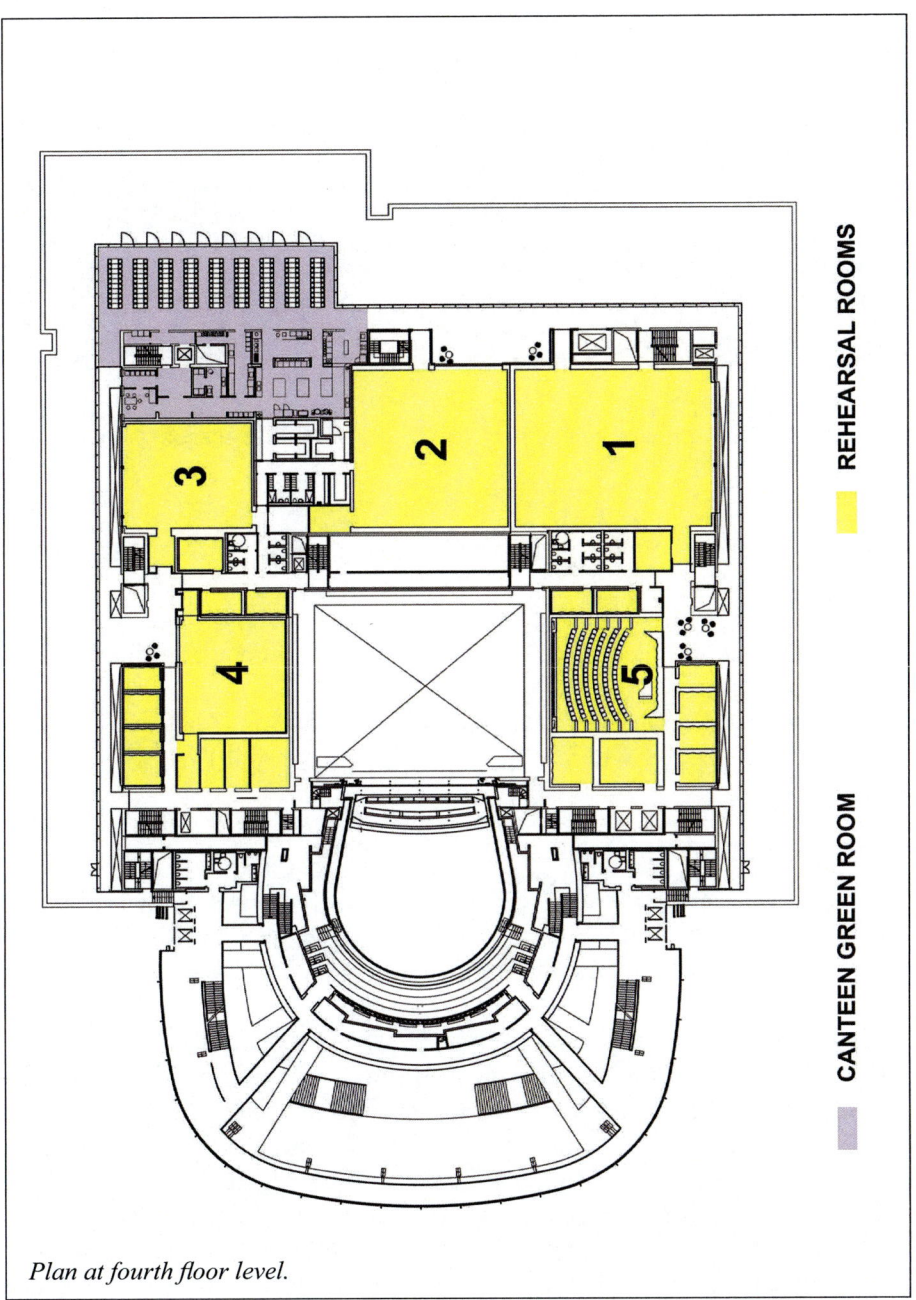

Plan at fourth floor level.

Copenhagen Opera House 25

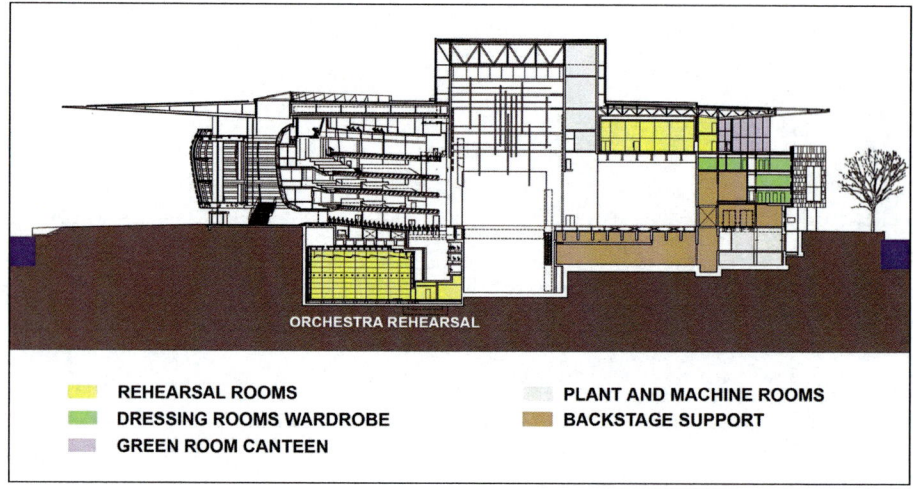

	REHEARSAL ROOMS		PLANT AND MACHINE ROOMS
	DRESSING ROOMS WARDROBE		BACKSTAGE SUPPORT
	GREEN ROOM CANTEEN		

The open corridors enable artists, and especially guest artists, to orientate easily and quickly.

Rehearsal rooms for choir, soloists, singers and ballet dancers are placed on the fourth floor under the massive roof structure with a magnificent view across the harbour to the city.

The staff canteen is also located on the fourth floor, and has an extensive outdoor roof terrace which offers a fantastic view all the way to the Øresundsbroen.

Royal Box
The royal box is placed on the left side of the auditorium, according to tradition. It has direct access to the private royal lounge which the Queen and her guests use on arrival and during intervals.

Materials
Materials and colours have been chosen primarily from the light end of the colour scale in order to relate to the surroundings and to adhere to the simple Nordic traditions. The outdoor surfaces are sandstone, granite, metal and glass – emphasising the various building elements of the Opera.

The island podium is covered with natural stone with various surfaces. The plaza paving is Chinese granite, and the foyer flooring is Perlatino marble. The floating metal roof has a ribbed structure to add character to the extensive surface, which makes the Opera significant and easily recognisable from the air.

The facades of the main building are covered with natural Jura Gelb stone, which provides a beautiful, smooth surface – broken by bands of windows and narrow light slots. This is contrasted by the open foyer towards the harbour, the walls being mainly in glass, and the natural stone floor and the metal ceiling corresponding to the plaza and the roof. In addition, the two top levels have transparent glass facades which accentuate the floating roof. Auditorium materials are golden and dark stained maple, smoked oak and gold leaf.

4 THE ROLE OF THE THEATRE CONSULTANT

This was the ultimate role for a theatre consultant – to advise a team of building design professionals on all aspects of the creation, planning, designing, equipping, fitting-out and setting to work of a 21st century opera house. The professional design team certainly had experience; architects Henning Larsens Tegnestue and engineers Rambøll from Denmark both have extensive international portfolios, but not in the area of theatre. The other main member of the team, Arup Acoustics, had considerable theatre experience and were very helpful in supporting us and the 'performing art' when things got a bit difficult! Rambøll sought specialist assistance in the early stages of the project from engineers Buro Happold from Glasgow who had worked on a number of UK theatres. Our client for the project was the AP Møller and Chastine Mc-Kinney Møller Foundation.

The architects were already appointed when I was called for interview with the Foundation whilst on holiday in Crete in 2000. I made arrangements to get to Copenhagen as promptly as possible but with no real brief other than that there were plans for an opera house. My nervousness at attending such an important interview with nothing prepared was increased significantly when the PA who led me into the empty conference room started by lowering the blinds, saying, "You can plug your computer in there and use the lectern!" I got the blinds raised again and, after the initial introductions round the table, asked for a briefing.

From there things went positively. We had an open discussion about what was planned, what they felt was needed, what we could offer and about the time such a project might take. I was also asked about acousticians with experience of designing opera houses as Arup Acoustics had not, at that time, been appointed. The approach of the Foundation to this interview was quite understandable; let the architect and others get to grips with the visitor and then if thought worth it, bring in the artillery. Thus when Mr Ib Kruse, who was in charge of the project for Mr Maersk Møller, joined the meeting I began to get into difficulty. Based on my previous theatre construction experience in many countries I did not believe that we could proceed from having no detailed brief to handing over a finished fully-functioning opera house in less than five years. In some countries that would be a miracle. But I didn't at that stage know the Foundation. This interview was in October 2000 and I was told firmly that Mr Møller required the opera project to be complete by 1st October 2004.

I explained something of what was required to get an opera house planned and the time it can take to get approvals and funding, and the time needed to create a high-class auditorium and to design and specify all the technical installations. I then described the extensive testing and commissioning involved and the need to have everything organised like a military operation. This was all obviously taken on board along with my proposals as to how the time scale could be shortened, and I was advised that there would be no funding delays and that matters needing decisions would be dealt with very promptly. The Foundation would have a full-time project director, Bo Wildfang, a team at the AP Møller headquarters and a full-time project manager on site, Peter Poulsen. The chemistry must have been working because I was told that Mr Maersk Møller would like to meet me that afternoon.

Following a very pleasant discussion with this amazing entrepreneur who was then 88 years old and who asked some very shrewd questions about opera and opera houses, I departed with the positive feeling of an interview which had gone well. Following a number of faxes and e-mails, the supplying of references and a visit by the Foundation to see our work in the Gran Teatre del Liceu in Barcelona and the Royal Opera House, Covent Garden, a number of them came, with the architects, to our offices in Kingston. That was a bit of a full house but this time they got a full PowerPoint presentation! We received notification of our appointment at the end of November, leaving three years and 10 months to complete the project.

We exchanged many documents, including scopes of work and draft contracts, before we finally signed an agreement, but that did not stop the work commencing before Christmas in 2000. One of the first things was to get to know the architects and engineers and try to establish a way of working that was acceptable to everyone. In meetings where two larger practices work in their own national way and, although speaking very good English, communicate more easily in Danish, setting the ground rules was not easy. It is important on any theatre-building project that everyone understands just what is required functionally as well as aesthetically. Also the unexpected has to be explained to those with no idea of what goes on in a theatre. I occasionally tell the story of a design for a significant UK project in which the engineers submitted drawings for the mechanical services with ducts running right through the flying space in the fly tower. We didn't have that problem, but we did have some other surprises down the line!

Theatreplan was retained to establish a likely programme for the use of the theatre in terms of the type of presentations (opera, ballet, dance, musicals, drama, concerts), the frequency of changeovers, time for fit-ups, rehearsals, extent of in-house services and similar, and then to prepare a full Brief for the opera house and its operations in descriptive terms. This was fine and proper but what was interesting was that we were to do this without any contact with the Royal Theatre, the main Danish theatre company which, it was anticipated, would be taking over the Opera when it was completed. This was quite a task and required considerable research and consideration. The Foundation provided the background to an original Government scheme for an opera house and other data that they had obtained in their discussions with Government and with the Royal Theatre. But we were asked to prepare what was needed in a perfect world rather than what the Royal Theatre might feel that they wanted.

In summary the requirement was for the presentation of opera and ballet in repertoire over most of the year with the ability to stage other lyric or musical shows for a period in the summer. The house was to accommodate the full opera company and orchestra, and the ballet company as visitors. The building was to provide full rehearsal and practice facilities and wardrobe and scenery repair shops, but not accommodate the making of costumes or the construction of properties or scenery as these would be made in the existing Royal Theatre workshops. The Royal were also planning a new complex with larger workshops and central storage on a site outside Copenhagen.

Other important tasks included confirming the number of seats and the likely form of the auditorium, the size of the stalls area, number of balconies and the size and adaptability of the orchestra pit, these aspects being planned in

Clive Odom of Theatreplan explaining the intricacies of the orchestra pit in a design team meeting.

collaboration with the architects and acousticians. The largest size of the orchestra pit and its effect on distancing the performers from their audience and the way the orchestra would use the pit was, as usual, a major consideration.

The stage planning had to take account of the need to present heavy scenic shows in repertoire. It was clear from the early sketches tabled by the architects that the requirement for side and rear stages was understood but the methods by which scenery would be brought in, erected and moved around had to be explained. Then there was the need to establish as soon as practicable the maximum and minimum sizes of the proscenium opening and the base sight lines so that the correct dimensions for the stage area could be determined. It is interesting to note that there are a number of theatres where the basic masking of the stage is not considered early enough and the fly tower is built insufficiently wide or the galleries are too far onstage for the proscenium opening.

In parallel with this Theatreplan had to prepare a full Schedule of Accommodation and a set of relationship diagrams to help everyone on the design team to see how all the ancillary accommodation could be located around the auditorium and stage. In the theatre technical disciplines, Theatreplan had full responsibility for the stage engineering, stage and work lighting, sound, video and performance communications, although some aspects of the design and specific purchases reverted to the Royal Theatre later in the project after the form of the building, its facilities and accommodation, and the technical budget, were all established. This is a practice Theatreplan encourage where there is a professional user client: designers and technical crew often have personal preferences as to the luminaires, mixing consoles, intercom systems and other items that they would like to use and it is beneficial to the project to work with the users to design a suitable infrastructure and for the users finally to select such plug-in items as are appropriate.

The tight project timescale was generally maintained during the design period although the project manager did have to push the design team at the end of the detail design period when the usual difficult areas of the orchestra pit and ceiling in the auditorium were not being finalised as rapidly as was necessary. Some three months were scheduled for the preparation of the brief and for outline design; this was followed by a conceptual design period of three months, design proposals (scheme design) in three-and-a-half months, with detail design taking another two-and-a-half months. Thus all the principle decisions were to be made within a year. Production information was scheduled to be available by mid-July 2002, some 19 months after commencement. Work started on preparing the site in advance so that it was ready for construction of the deep basements to start in September 2002.

This put a lot of pressure on the Theatreplan team but the clear instructions that we were to make our own recommendations based on our knowledge and experience did help. In the early stages there were many changes of direction and our original schedule of accommodation did not get immediate endorsement. It recommended the inclusion of a restaurant for the public and a studio theatre, neither of which were considered important by the Foundation at the time. Theatres in Copenhagen did not entertain visitors except for the performance and the idea of having the foyers open during the day was not really welcomed. There was a similar reaction to the idea of a bookshop selling theatrical merchandise. Neil Morton and I stressed that the Opera was going to be one of the most important and most visited buildings in Denmark and needed to provide such facilities. Fortunately these features were reconsidered and facilities for day-time visitors have been included. Even before the opening some 22,000 people had booked, and paid for, a conducted tour of the building and thousands had reserved tables in the top foyer restaurant for a meal.

It was also necessary to explain the need for a studio theatre. As people in the theatre know, it is vital to have a space where new writing, new work, new actors and new directors can be tried out. Such work and smaller scale productions can go on to lead to some of the great masterpiece performances. A studio also allows for more intimate productions, chamber opera and small modern dance and ballet works which will be welcomed by a specialist audience but could not fill the main house. We discovered later that the Royal Theatre also wanted a smaller venue for lectures and master classes. Unfortunately the original Government brief was not prepared by a theatre consultant and did not reflect this need, so it was difficult for the Foundation to extend their gift to include such a space. It is a great credit to them that a studio stage was included in the scheme and developed right through to the end, although it did suffer some considerable uphill battles in the course of its gestation.

The major issue, as on so many projects, was that the footprint of the building and the area given in the schedule of accommodation exceeded that of what were thought of as 'comparable' projects. This required a lot of explanations and reasoned arguments to the Foundation in conjunction with the architects. The problem is that it is very difficult to find truly comparable arts projects anywhere in the world to the one you are trying to create. As part of the concept stage, the architects arranged a number of visits to specific venues, to help the client and design team appreciate both their architectural approach and also understand the background to some historic and current theatres. In addition to these, detailed examinations of the built areas of a number of other opera houses were made from plans, as the information available by other means was not always considered reliable. The final Schedule of Accommodation, on the basis of which the design was developed, had a net building area of some 19,684 sq metres. When grossed up to allow for plant, corridors, lifts, stairs, ducts and wall thicknesses, this became a gross figure of 31,356 sq metres.

From our studies and experience, we were aware that the intended repertoire could only be presented efficiently if there were spaces provided for the erection of sets and where operas could be rehearsed with the complete built setting. Ideas developed on other projects also came into play: the idea of storing a complete dance floor for ballet constructed on a wagon under the rear stage was one of these. Then you have to decide whether this 750 mm high storage slot, like the area of the grid, is a measurable floor area to be included in the schedule of accommodation. There is no profession of quantity surveying in Denmark and there were days when I would have given anything for a UK cost consultant to have joined the team. The initial cost plan was developed by the architects and engineers, with that for the stage engineering, lighting, sound and communications being prepared by Theatreplan.

Apart from the increase in area, the cost of the technical installations became an issue. Despite having completed the Royal Opera House the previous year, the figures prepared by Jeff Phillips, Clive Odom and myself were considered high compared with other 'comparable' theatres. One of these theatres we knew quite a lot about: the Gran Teatre del Liceu in Barcelona. We also knew the way in which the tenders had been sought: quite an interesting approach in which you submit the drawings and Employer's Requirements and indicate the figure at which you want the tender returned. Contractors with strong nerves price the job on what it will cost and take the risk that no-one else is hungry. Otherwise they go in at, or just below, the indicated cost, in either case expecting to find due reason to claim the necessary extras! In fact the contractor who won the Barcelona project, Waagner Biro, negotiated a number of changes and omissions in order that the project could be completed at around the bid price. While a very comprehensive installation, it doesn't reflect all the facilities that had been specified and did not really equate to what was required in Copenhagen. The stage engineering costs were only some 75% of what we had calculated was needed in Copenhagen. In fact Copenhagen was technically far more comparable with Covent Garden than with Barcelona.

Another 'comparable' project that was visited a couple of times was the Finnish National Opera in Helsinki. Opened in 1992, this opera house includes full wardrobe and workshop facilities but only has side and rear stages with wagons and a further scenery storage space in the basement. The building has a great ambience in both public and backstage areas and a number of the excellent details of the sort that you point out to architects during a tour! The accommodation in the building is generous in planning terms, but with the exception of the stage and side stage areas. The stage is unfortunately not wide enough to allow full off-stage masking, a pretty important issue when planning an opera house. Also, the stage equipment installation in Helsinki was always quoted to us as representing what we should aim for, but this was a far lower cost figure than we knew would be tenable in 2003-4 in Copenhagen. We were also rather concerned about some features of the Helsinki stage engineering installations which we considered inappropriate for a major state opera house. Only after considerable investigation did we discover that these stage equipment installations had been specified by the suppliers, of which there were five, only one of whom had theatre experience. We later discovered that of the five contractors, three had gone into liquidation after the completion of the opera. The Finnish State Opera is now being upgraded to eliminate many of these functional and operational limitations and to provide an up-to-date stage engineering installation.

The cost of the technical installations was not the only fiscal item that had to be resolved; on a performing arts complex there are many apparent 'extravagances' which always need to be explained. Agreement was reached on the final cost plan for the building during the detail design phase and although there were some tenders received for technical equipment above the individual estimated figures, the total expenditure in this discipline was just under the budget figure. Both the client and Theatreplan were very pleased with this result as other budgets were exceeded, in some areas possibly due to the detailed theatrical requirements not being fully understood in the early stages of the project.

After concept design our role as theatre consultants proceeded along two parallel paths, with the backstage planning and auditorium design being led by Neil Morton and the stage area planning and technical installations being directed by myself. As close a liaison as possible was maintained between the two teams which often came together with the architects and acousticians to resolve the usual critical areas, such as where to place the control rooms and to locate lighting positions and loudspeakers throughout the auditorium. The proscenium zone was especially complex and required all-party understanding and co-operation on the orchestra pit, stage front and architectural proscenium. Neil worked with Liam Hennessy on the auditorium design and Liam spent periods in Henning Larsen's offices working up the seating and sightline details for the architects. Leandro Rotondi prepared the 700 or so sightline studies that we did in order to ensure that the position and view from every seat was as good as possible. The work they undertook in all these areas is more fully described in Chapter 5.

The technical team consisted of Clive Odom, David Ludlam and myself on stage engineering, John Whitaker and Mike Atkinson on stage and work lighting systems and Charles Wass working with Rick Clarke and Eric Pressley on sound, video and communications. While for much of the project these specialisations each followed their own course, they came together in certain areas, such as when it was proposed to eliminate the multi-circuit feeds to the overstage lighting and use distributed dimmers on the flown lighting frames. Another difficult co-ordination exercise, which included the architects and acousticians, was when trying to accommodate loudspeakers to provide coverage of the auditorium from within the moving architectural proscenium. The principles behind the installations employed in each of these disciplines are set out in separate chapters.

All in all the Opera Project was a very rewarding experience with the best client of my 38-year long theatre-consulting career. Our role was generally respected and our decisions endorsed. In addition to the natural friendliness and acceptance offered by the Danes, we had positive on-site project management and a supportive contract management team with which to complete a serious project in an extremely short time. There were the 'down' days and decisions we didn't understand but generally it was a very forward-looking operation right from day one. And we were pleased with the contractors' contributions and with their tenders. In fact, while we kept a record of the main variations to the technical contracts, it was the managing contractors, E Pihl and Søn, who kept saying that as far as they were concerned our work was within the overall technical budget and they even produced figures that confirmed this!

5 THE DEVELOPMENT OF THE AUDITORIUM
Neil Morton, Richard Brett

Theatreplan collaborated with Henning Larsens Tegnestue (HLT) and Arup Acoustics in the design of the auditorium. The short timescale for the whole project established by the Client meant that there was great pressure to establish the design of the auditorium right from the start. The time allowed for developing the auditorium concept from the completion of the Brief was only a matter of a few weeks. Henning Larsen's team had previously won the architectural competition for the Compton Verney Opera House in the UK working with Richard Brett and others, and were intrigued with the possibility of designing the Copenhagen auditorium in the traditional 'horseshoe' form. A strategic decision had to be made rapidly whether to pursue a modern interpretation of this form or whether to explore a different approach. The other important member of the design team, Arup Acoustics, had achieved great success with the Glyndebourne Opera House and was keen to develop an evolution of the horseshoe form. It was therefore decided early on that the team should explore alternatives within the horseshoe form although, given more time, Theatreplan would have relished the opportunity to explore more radical approaches.

Two study trips to look at historical and contemporary opera auditoria in Europe were undertaken by senior members of the design team with representatives of the Client. Such trips are vital in

The design team in Staatsoper, Vienna.

establishing common ground, as a basis for the discussion of both theatrical and design matters within the professional team and with the client. Such shared experiences can inform and thus simplify many of the decisions during design development. Visits were made to Opèra National de Lyon, Teatro Farnese in Parma, Teatro Municipale Valli in Reggio Emilia, La Scala in Milan, and to both the Staatsoper and Teater an der Wien in Vienna. The trip to Lyon was to examine a modern interpretation of multi-tier opera house and indicated both the qualities in terms of proportions, and the difficulties in terms of sightlines, associated with the height of the room. It was also interesting to experience a room with all black finishes except for the golden-coloured house curtain and the crimson-lined sound and light locks. The architects were excited by the purity of La Scala, but appreciated the sightline limitations imposed by the boxes and the remoteness of the upper tiers. Vienna illustrated a 1950s rebuilding of the original auditorium. When it was rebuilt the tiers and seating were adjusted to take account of the changes in social structure of a 20th century audience and therefore reflected more closely the requirements of a contemporary room.

Visits were also arranged to Glyndebourne, the Royal Opera House, Covent Garden and to Helsinki Opera. These visits led to a common awareness of the challenges of building a theatre in this form with modern levels of comfort and with the sight line expectations of a modern audience. Helsinki also demonstrated the problems of balancing comfort and sightlines from side seats. One aspect that was being debated at the time of the visits was the dominance of an entrance on the central axis of an auditorium. The opera houses visited showed several approaches to a central rear entrance and the separation of an audience caused by a central aisle.

Teatro Farnese Parma.

Royal Opera House, Covent Garden.

Glyndebourne auditorium.

The team in Helsinki Opera.

The seating capacity was officially set at 1400 which is quite small for an opera house. In view of the cost of staging opera and the generous site available, Theatreplan suggested that perhaps consideration should be given to designing a larger theatre seating around 1800. The existing Royal Theatre Old Stage (Gamle Scene) in Copenhagen has a capacity of around 1300 seats. Both Arup Acoustics and Theatreplan felt that 1800 represented the maximum seating numbers with which it was possible to achieve intimacy and good audience contact, as well as satisfactory acoustics. The Client felt very strongly that a smaller number was right to ensure a full and popular building and was happy to proceed with a number closer to 1400. In order to ensure realising this number, the design pursued by Theatreplan aimed at slightly higher than 1400 so that, when all the difficulties of ensuring good sightlines were overcome, the team would be sure of achieving at least this number of good seats.

The five tiers of La Scala, Milan.

The five tiers of Nouvel Opéra in Lyon.

A vital early matter was to consider the number of tiers. It was felt that the two tiers and stalls circle of the smaller capacity Glyndebourne lacked the intensity of traditional houses like La Scala with five tiers and stalls circle and Covent Garden with three tiers and stalls circle. This together with the intimacy required suggested that three tiers would be more appropriate. Consideration was given to more tiers but the lessons learnt from the height of the upper tiers in Lyon had cautioned against placing the audience too high in the room. Three tiers for audience appeared to offer the balance between height and spacing required and was the form finally developed. A fourth technical tier was introduced so that the overall spatial form and proportion of the room was more comparable to a traditional house. The total capacity of the auditorium with a normal opera-size orchestra pit is 1468 which reduces to 1436 for productions with the largest orchestra pit. With no orchestra pit the seating capacity rises to 1647. The auditorium stalls area seats 775, reducing to 594 or 562 with different pit sizes. The first tier seats 266, the second 315 and the top tier accommodates 291 with a further 56 standing places.

The architects sought to find an expression for the auditorium that was fresh and provided a connection with the city beyond the boundaries of the building. The idea of continuing the external plaza directly into the foyers and onto the terracing of the stalls held a strong fascination for them. In many ways this is not dissimilar to Utzon's approach with the stalls rake being an extension of the external terracing in Sydney Opera House. This led to the idea of trying to express the auditorium as a floating pumpkin-like form hovering above the plane of the stalls, the main foyer and the external plaza. In order to fully realise this concept of the foyer and plaza flowing through into the auditorium HLT wished to create as large door openings as possible at the rear of the stalls. The

The audience awaits.

Concept sketches by Troel Troelsen of HLT.

expression of the external form is carried forward into the philosophy for the interior of room. The desire to maintain this clarity of architectural expression, together with the desire to optimise the number of forward facing seats, influenced the decision to develop a scheme without a separate stalls circle level. The interior of the room was conceived on the idea that the inner space within the auditorium was carved out of the solid pumpkin form.

The challenge of the idea of continuing the plaza through to the stalls area was how to balance this with the difference in levels, the need for large acoustic doors, and how to provide control rooms with adequate

The plaza and foyer entrances.

Copenhagen Opera House 41

sightlines. HLT wanted to minimise the number of steps up into the auditorium and, preferably, to have none. Many contemporary and historic theatres have stage, backstage and the stalls foyer at the same level for ease of access to all parts of the building. In order to provide a steeper stalls rake than many traditional houses some steps up are therefore required to reach the level at the rear of the stalls. The stage and backstage levels in Copenhagen had been established to suit the natural site levels. Raising the plaza as a horizontal plane this far above grade to meet the level of the rear stalls was impracticable. As a possible solution HLT investigated making the foyers and plaza as a sloping plane, rising gently up from the water level to the level required for the rear stalls. A section of sloping floor was mocked-up in the HLT office and meetings held on this sloping section to evaluate the effect of moving around and standing on a raked plane. After this trial, a client decision was made to maintain a flat foyer. This led to the necessity of steps up into the main entrances at rear of the stalls. Access which is level with the foyer is available at each side of the auditorium for wheelchairs. The side aisles of the auditorium are ramped allowing wheelchairs to be accommodated in several positions within the auditorium. The stalls seating is placed on horizontal levels forming each row, these being just above the ramped plane of the aisles, with a small step into each row of seats.

There was much debate as to the number of steps from the foyer to the rear of the stalls that would be acceptable. The minimum number was important to the architects who wanted the audience standing in foyer to be able to see over the seats through to the stage. This decision led to extensive sightline studies to examine the effects of slightly reducing the stalls rake below that initially recommended by Theatreplan in order to the minimise the impact of these steps and maintain to concept of the connection with the foyers.

An important acoustic consideration was to ensure that energy coming from a singer on stage is not immediately absorbed by the seated audience. For this reason a shallow stalls rake is beneficial acoustically as it allows the energy to build in the space in a similar manner to the way this occurs in the majority of historic theatres.

Stalls side aisle and seating.

The importance of maintaining this energy had to be re-understood by learning the lesson from the failures of some of the modernist designs built in the 1930s, 40s, and 50s. The decision to proceed with a shallow rake was discussed with the client and the Royal Theatre and appreciation of the limitations on sightlines for dance was fully understood.

Increased seat numbers at the lower level were achieved by not having a stalls circle or parterre. As a result the effective seated area in the room is wider and can have longer rows. The requirement of having the auditorium apparently floating above the base level also contributed to the decision not to have a stalls circle. Maximising the width of the central entrance also meant it was difficult to place the control rooms at the rear of the stalls. After the consideration of many options, it was decided that it was best to locate a full suite of control rooms together at the rear of the first tier. This was considered better than splitting them and placing them far from the centre on either side at the rear of the stalls. The available rear stalls positions have been developed into an extra booth each side which can be used for audio description, directors, stage management, surtitle operations and other functions.

Det Kongelige Teater, Copenhagen.

The existing Royal Theatre is a very intimate room and there was awareness within the design team that it would be difficult to achieve a similar degree of intimacy with the increased seating numbers and much better natural acoustics which were key principles in the design brief for the new opera. The Royal Theatre has electronically-assisted acoustics to increase the clarity and the reverberation within the room. In the design of the new auditorium it was important to find increased volume both at the rear and high in the room, whilst closing down the scale at the front, towards the stage, in order to maintain intimacy. One of the difficulties posed in the design of a contemporary house is the impact of improving the acoustics of the seats under the overhang at the rear of the tiers. This leads to increased spacing of the tiers and the side balconies. This increased vertical spacing changes the scale of the room and much of the intensity formed by closeness of the side balconies that create the magic of an Italian opera house. The proximity and contact between the audience and performer at the sides of the room is important to retain.

Formally the idea of straight horizontal balconies is appealing but if followed through from the heights required at the rear, they are too widely spaced to achieve the scale and contact of the traditional horseshoe houses. Early in the design of the auditorium a decision was made by the Danish royal family and the client that the royal box should remain in a similar position on the Konge side of the house as in the existing Royal Theatre. This is on the left side of the auditorium in Scandinavia which is the opposite side to English tradition. In developing the design Theatreplan were determined to bring the side tier incorporating the royal box as low and as close to the stage as possible. As a result, the Queen and the royal guests are sitting only just above the performer's eye line. All these considerations led to a room with sloping side tiers. The front of the first circle is lower than the equivalent seating in Covent Garden.

The slope of the balconies has benefits for the sightlines in the main tiers and has

The Royal Box.

made it possible to increase the rake at the sides and allows the rear rows to be horizontal or even to rake slightly upwards. Gently-sloping balconies to improve the sightlines at the side are commonly seen in the work carried out by Frank Matcham in England at the beginning of the 20th century. The introduction of raised levels in the slips at the sides also helped to reduce the scale.

The three tiers and technical level above.

The large acoustic volume required in an opera house results in a high ceiling leaving a lot of space above the third tier level. A fourth technical tier was introduced which is similar in appearance to the audience tiers below to help counteract both the apparent widening of the room at this level and also to reduce the overall height of the room. The fourth tier has a full balcony front but actually masks a technical and lighting position right around the auditorium.

Estimates of the numbers of seats were compiled as sketches of concepts of the room were created. This is a notoriously difficult procedure and can often lead to over-estimates of seating numbers. As soon as was practicable, Theatreplan began producing more detailed seating layouts to check the numbers, although because of the way that the project was developing these were often rapidly superseded. Design of an auditorium is an extremely time-consuming iterative process. Even when it may appear to be reaching a conclusion architecturally, it is necessary to check and recheck levels and sightlines. A change in level as small as 50mm or 100mm may have an exponential effect on the levels higher in the room. The affects of small changes need to be checked for their impact on sightlines, acoustics, and aisle ramps and steppings. All require very careful consideration.

There are many techniques used by those experienced in designing auditoria. These have to be understood and the application of them accepted by both architect and the local building regulatory authorities. The Danish building codes as applied to auditoria did impose some limitations. The regulation relating to balcony rail height would have made the construction of the higher tiers impractical due to the effect of these rails on the sightlines. Fortunately, by being involved in the discussions with the authorities, Theatreplan was able to examine with them how the balcony rails worked in the existing Royal Theatre and the impact higher rails would have on sightlines. Examples of how the detailing of theatre balcony rails have developed in various countries were discussed. After these investigations they accepted the UK regulation height of 790mm which is lower than in some countries, as they shared the problem and understood how important a low-height rail was to achieving proper and acceptable sightlines in a multi-tier theatre.

Detailed sightline studies began as soon as the design of the auditorium design reached a point where such 3D modeling could realistically assist. Computer simulations of the view to stage were created for every seating position in which it was anticipated, from experience, that sightlines could be critical. These not only covered side and rear seats but also many seats in the main parts of the stalls and tiers in order to check the views to the stage floor, to the conductor and also to a surtitle screen. These led to the examination of many options at the sides of the tiers where conventional rows of seats, if continued down the sides of the house, have to rise significantly and become very unsatisfactory. The introduction of level slips (boxes) and a raised side gallery proved the best solution. The location of these boxes needed careful coordination with the structure of the level above to ensure headroom and suitable upward sightlines.

Sightline studies also confirm issues like the height the control room floor needs to be at to be above the rear of that in the tier in front and the positions from which it is not practicable to see the surtitle screen. As these developed it was possible to achieve good viewing from the control rooms at the rear of the first tier, even if the sound team did want to be able to open their control room window and push the sound desk out into the auditorium over the rear row of seats! While the opinion was expressed that not all seats needed to view the surtitles, the impracticability of determining who would select such seats pushed for the decision to provide some repeater screens for the seats with a restricted view of the main surtitle screen. The surtitle system contractor developed a compact repeater screen which could be mounted in either the seat back of the row in front, or in boxes that hinged out from the box front and could be adjusted to the optimum angle for easy viewing. The seating contractor provided a cable route through the necessary chairs and fitted the screens in the seat backs. Larger repeater screens were fitted to the rear rail

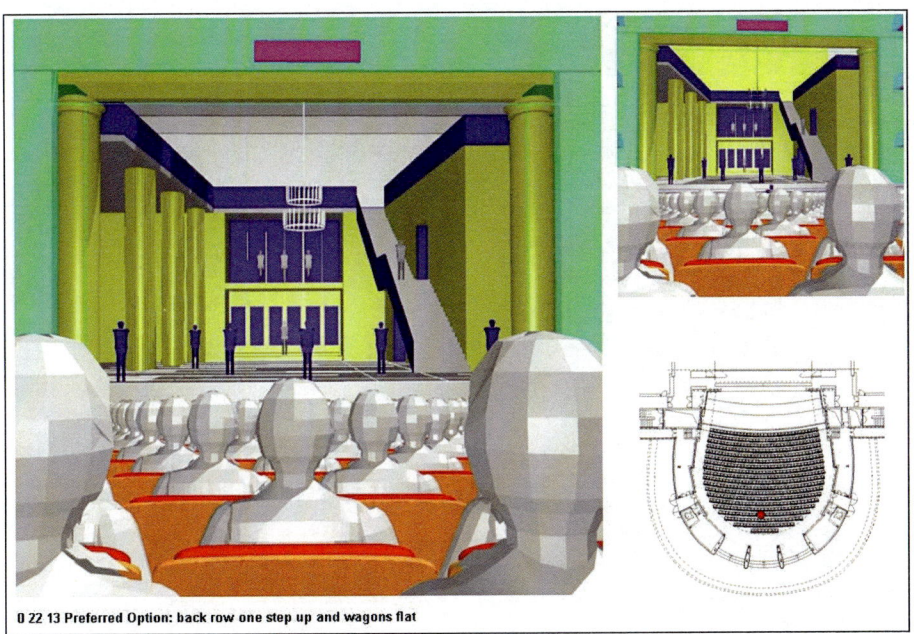

0 22 13 Preferred Option: back row one step up and wagons flat

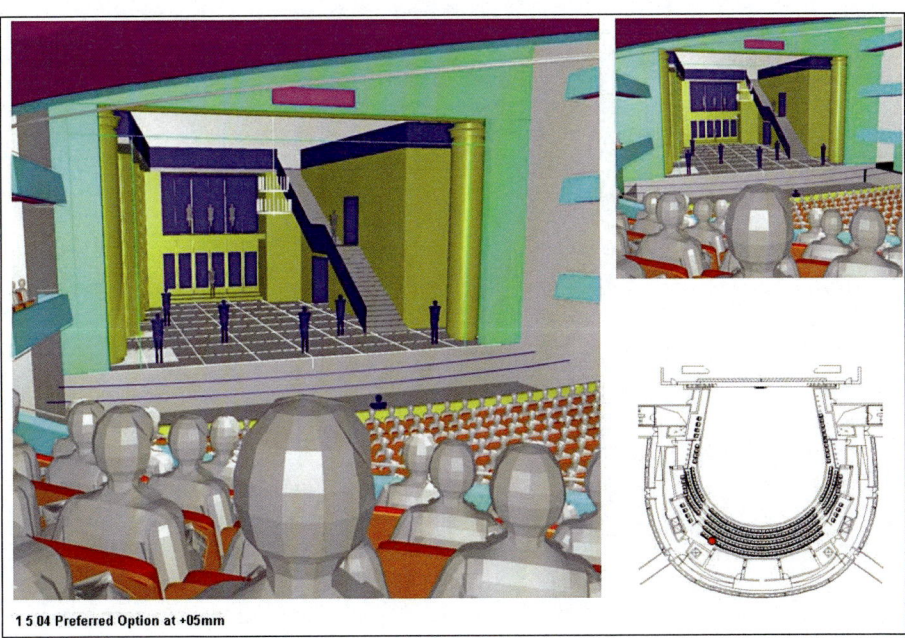

1 5 04 Preferred Option at +05mm

Copenhagen Opera House

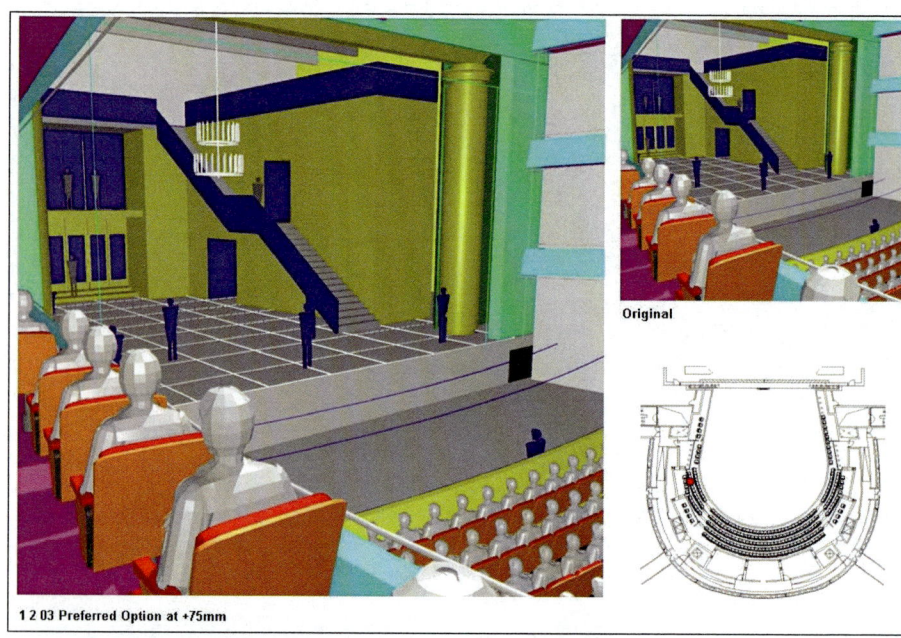

1 2 03 Preferred Option at +75mm
Original

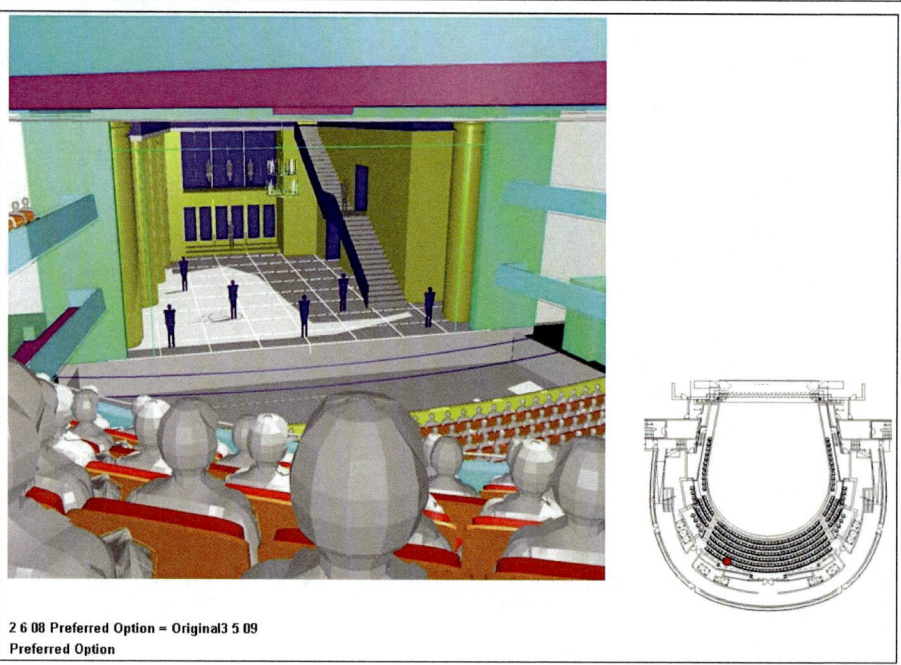

2 6 08 Preferred Option = Original3 5 09
Preferred Option

of the technical tier to provide a clear view of the surtitles for the rear row in the third tier and the standing row behind. Out of the maximum of 1468 seats only 180 or 12% needed repeater screens.

The side seating in many opera houses and other modern theatres is often not satisfactory. In some that were visited the seats had been positioned around the side as an extension of the front row such that one could not see without leaning forward to the rail. This was not comfortable because of the width of the circulation space needed in front of the seat for access. A conscious decision was made to make the sightlines from the side seating as good as possible and this was made at the expense of maximising the number of people seated at the sides. The relatively small capacity required for this house helped this decision. In order to achieve good sightlines and comfort in the side seats, the seats were turned to face the stage with the side of the seat against the balcony front. This gives both the clearest view of the stage and the greatest seated comfort, with very little twisting or leaning. On the visit to Glyndebourne it was noticed that the side seating there had been changed, after the opening season, from being forward facing (perpendicular to the balcony front and facing towards the centre of the auditorium) to be as in Copenhagen, facing the stage along the line of the balcony.

A second row of seating was introduced as a set of slips (boxes) at a higher level behind the side seating in the tiers. In order to ensure these seats worked most effectively it was necessary to minimise the width of the aisle to the front row. After examining many mock ups the space necessary for the front side aisle was minimised and these side seats are installed without arms. The

The side seats on the third tier.

Side slip boxes at first tier level.

People occupying the slip boxes on the second tier.

seats are still comfortable and easy to access.

The row spacing and legroom was examined with the client at an early stage using a mock-up of possible seats and a section of balcony front. These mock-ups were developed using very slim seating forms with hard backs and thin cushions to maximise the space available. The seats used were based on a standard seat from a UK manufacturer. The row-to-row spacing selected was a balance between comfort and overall scale of the space. This is typically 900mm but varies slightly in some locations. The seating mock-ups were built with different width seats and with different back angles in short rows with a section of balcony front in order to ensure that the client and whole design team were happy with the details before the development of the room design was undertaken.

From this study, and perhaps partially because it was set up in a warehouse in winter without heating and the occupants were wearing coats, the decision was made to use a slightly wider seats than originally planned. In most theatres three sizes of seats are typically used to set up the rows and to align the row ends. In Copenhagen just two widths were used, 540mm and 560mm. Special provision was made for the shaping of the balcony front to allow extra space for toes so as not to increase the aisle width and restrict the sightlines with the balcony rail.

The seating mock-up in steep rake format.

HLT were very keen to develop a unique seat for the project. Everyone agreed that a pedestal seat was the best form as it would minimise fixings and simplify the setting out. A single pedestal was also more suitable for fixing on the sloping levels on the balcony tiers. The first sketches for the seat were drawn by a Danish furniture designer working closely with HLT. The actual production seat was later developed by Race Seating, a UK manufacturer, working with the architects and an industrial designer employed by the seating company.

An interesting idea from the development of the seat was a pedestal design for the stalls which is easily removed without bolts so that disabled positions, production desks and television cameras could easily be set up. Once the design for this had been developed, the seat manufacturer suggested that it would be no more expensive to use these seats throughout the stalls area. It was agreed to go with this as it expedited installation and makes replacing a damaged seat extremely easy. It also offered potential to have a performance with a standing audience for special events in the summer season. A performance in this mode would reinforce the concept of the link through from the plaza, into the foyers and on to the stalls terracing. The seat design also has a unique device for adjusting the back and arm positions in a single mechanism. This is vital in a three-tier house for achieving the correct angle for the backs in each tier so as to position the audience comfortably for their view to the stage.

Interestingly, the choice of seat fabric, a difficult decision in any project, took far longer than had been expected due to the difficulty of determining the balance between materials, quality, wearing-properties, colour, acoustic performance, effect of lighting and so on. After many trials, investigations and mock-ups the client was finally willing to make a decision on the fabric to use.

The balcony fronts in any opera auditorium play a vital function in defining

Stalls seating.

Removable seats in the stalls.

Gala night with television camera in stalls.

the scale of the room as well as providing a surface which has an important role in creating the acoustics of the room. A challenge in a curved auditorium is to ensure that the curved form does not focus the sound reflected from the balcony fronts directly back to the stage. The balcony fronts need to be shaped so as to send energy from the sides back into the centre of the auditorium, whilst dispersing the potentially focussed energy into the room. This was achieved successfully in Glyndebourne and a similar approach was adopted for Copenhagen. More of the story of the acoustic design of the auditorium is given in Chapter 7.

The design goal was to achieve a harmonious and smooth balcony front form in all positions around its length in a way in appeared natural. Many hours were spent with drawings showing sections taken through the room every 10° in plan. Models were made and tested and finally sections of the shape were mocked up full size and examined. In order to eliminate heavy lighting rails and other technical features, cable routes are all inside and accessible through removable panels at the rear. Connectors pass through openings which are part of the aesthetic design, some of which contain lights and some incorporate hinged metal support arms for lighting and similar equipment. These are illustrated in Chapter 10.

In developing the auditorium ceiling, one of the aims was the necessity of creating a coordinated design for both stage lighting and acoustics that did not require large holes in the curved plane required for sound reflections which would also have destroyed the overall aesthetic form. Many options were explored by the architects, including a tensioned-wire grid with acoustic reflecting panels, and from these the client selected the more solid ceiling option. The approach taken in developing this form was to create a grid of small openings for the stage lighting in order to avoid the division of the ceiling into separate sections with significant gaps between them.

The auditorium ceiling.

In many traditional opera houses the proscenium zone is occupied by elaborate boxes which create a sense of separation and of viewing the performance through a large and deep gilded picture frame. In contrast many more modern theatres, particularly in Germany have created a dark no-mans land in this zone between the stage and the audience. One of the most interesting designs is Covent Garden which has a very minimal traditional proscenium that creates a contemporary relationship between the audience and performer. In developing the design for Copenhagen we wished to build on this idea by making the proscenium much more open and minimalist in order to break down any barriers in this zone. The zone is still dark to minimise any light spill and reflections, but the side balconies continue as far as practicable towards the stage. It also seemed right to explore opportunity to be able to dissolve the proscenium still further by opening the space up to be wide and large for a minimalist setting in which little or no awareness of the proscenium

The balconies extending to the proscenium in Copenhagen.

The tiers in the Royal Opera House meet the proscenium.

54 Copenhagen Opera House

is required. Thus the moving architectural proscenium was introduced to link the auditorium through to the stage more subtlety.

The architectural proscenium offers the facility to minimise the amount of black or dark surround apparent to an audience when the opera portal on-stage is closed in to create a smaller opening. This is achieved without the cost or complication of moving boxes or sidewalls. The architectural proscenium forms the main opening at the front of the stage but is part of the auditorium and employs the same, albeit, dark finishes near to the stage.

The near-stage side walls in Helsinki.

An associated challenge was to bring the side walls in close enough for acoustics and yet achieve the sense of the balconies continuing right to the stage. As the project developed the remaining space in the near-stage balconies was thought to be unacceptable for seating but with hindsight these positions could have included some more seats. Also during the design it was thought that the side seating might may be loose chairs, but it become clear as the building form developed that fixed seating would be more practicable, more comfortable and tidier. This decision was also affected by experience on other projects with loose seating, where it was noticed that people often did not put their seats in the most comfortable or best viewing positions.

Collaborating with Henning Larsens Tegnestue, Arup Acoustics and the engineers Ramboll AS on the design of this auditorium was a rewarding experience for all of us at Theatreplan. It is a credit to all members of the design team, and to those who interpreted the drawings and implemented the

A full house at Operaen.

construction and fitting out, that Operaen is such a successful example of a modern opera house offering great comfort, good sightlines and excellent acoustics.

6 THE STUDIO STAGE Richard Brett, Neil Morton

Very few arts buildings operate without a rehearsal room, studio or similar space in which smaller scale, more experimental works can be performed, as well as providing a space for master classes and other workshops. However, the original brief from the Danish Government for the opera house project did not include any such provision. The need for such a space was debated hotly during the preparation of the brief and then again during concept design phase. The client generously agreed to provide the additional performance space and it was decided that it should be on the first floor, above the truck loading bay, and below the canteen which was on the fourth level.

Theatreplan were convinced from day one that such a space was essential and that it should not be just another dumb black box. In this they were supported by the Royal Theatre and, for different reasons, by the architects who felt that the room should be another strong element in the massing of the opera house. HLT wanted to locate the studio on the rear of the building in order to bring a public face to the façade at the rear so that the opera house would relate in a more open manner to the existing community on Dock Island.

The nominal accommodation of the studio stage got recorded, as these things do, as being for an audience of 200 before the form or function of the space had been considered. In cost terms this meant 200 physical seats although no seating plan or different formats for performance had even been considered. The area of the room was large for 200 persons in order to provide the flexibility desired and, indeed,

Foyer to the studio stage seen above the loading bay doors.

Copenhagen Opera House 57

The separate public entrance to the studio stage foyer.

for a promenade performance or reception, twice that number could be easily accommodated. It was important that the 200 seats be provided in end stage mode. This results in higher seating capacities, around 260, for some of the more experimental formats. However, the number used for building code approval and for fire escape purposes was close to 200.

The height of the room was originally set with the architects at 11 metres to allow for two or three levels of audience and a technical space above, but this required the canteen to be higher than the other facilities on the fourth floor. These included the main rehearsal rooms, practice rooms and the chorus room. To eliminate the need for ramps and steps up into the canteen, the level of this area and of the kitchens was lowered, making the available studio height 10 metres. From this had to be deducted the space required for the sprung floor and the acoustic separation at ceiling level. The resulting 9.7 metres to the top of the structural beams is only just adequate. The structural beams had to be placed at exceptionally close centres to minimise their depth and thus maximise the clear height available.

It is interesting how many of these important 'development' spaces suffer a similar fate: both the Cottesloe in the National Theatre in London and the Linbury Studio in the Royal Opera House are examples that were accommodated in spaces with restricted height or other constraints which limits their full potential. The effect of this height reduction is most serious in the technical space at high-level which, apart from containing much of the overhead lighting, was also planned to accommodate some multi-line hoists and chain hoists above a tensioned-wire grid. At the sides the whole height is taken up with supply and extract air ducts. This results in a space in which it

The Canteen.

Above tensioned-wire grid during installation.

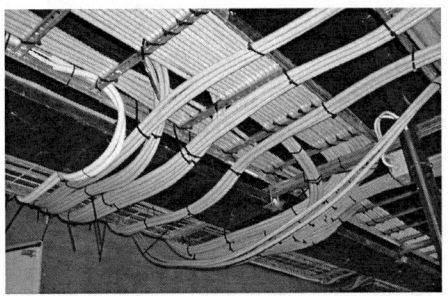
Cable routing in studio stage.

is difficult to stand upright and which has required some extremely tortuous wiring routes. It is actually a credit to all involved that the installations were completed at all, and while they are all workable, they are not as easy to use as the consultants had intended.

In order to provide for the widest range of activities, Neil Morton and the theatre planning team finally recommended an installation of retractable seating at the foyer end of the studio and a number of free-moving towers with two levels, both of which could take seated audience, the higher level forming a balcony. The towers were to be moved on air bearings so that they could be used to create a large number of audience and stage formats, and could also be removed entirely from the studio when not required. The retractable seating would provide a rapid method of accommodating an audience for a lunch-time lecture or master-class while the moveable towers would provide a very flexible space for other performances.

Models were made and shown, and real enthusiasm for the space began to be engendered. Then the cost of the towers was questioned; how many were there and why were these things called towers? They weren't in the architect's budget for the studio stage. 'Towers' is a general theatre term derived probably from the air-borne auditorium towers in the Derngate in Northampton, back in the 1970s. However the term confused our client and it was agreed that they

Towers being fabricated in the repertoire store on site.

would be formally called 'moving balcony units'. But how many were there to be and what would they cost remained the questions until the scheme was much further developed and all the alternatives could be considered.

Designing a studio stage which can take many formats is nearly as complicated as designing a major auditorium but this was not appreciated at the time either by the Foundation or by the architects. The engineers' commission didn't seem to extend to anything other than the main structure of the studio space although they were cajoled into preparing a design for the fixed technical gallery and later for the moving balcony units.

The architects also required a large window in the side wall of the studio to achieve their desire to link the auditorium with the community outside on Dock Island. They also decided to place this window on axis with one of the main streets on the island. In early consultations, the Royal Theatre also expressed their desire for daylight. Unfortunately locating the large window in this position did not relate comfortably with the layout of the theatre, especially in end stage format. The theatre consultants acknowledged that the activities in the studio stage might occasionally benefit from daylight, but they felt that having a large window with blackout curtains was a recipe for disaster. The acousticians also expressed concerns and ultimately the opening was reduced in size and replaced by high, hinged doors which improved the sound separation to the

Studio stage on the right showing the open doors behind the window.

foyers but still allowed for access and circulation for non-theatrical events.

The room was planned to have good access to the back stage on both of its axes and large sound-reducing doors to the scene dock were provided on the long side and the short side. The towers can be moved through these doors when not all are required, which allows for great flexibility in the staging.

Some 16 different formats were designed using the moving balcony units and the seating to create alternative performance spaces. These ranged from a recital room for chamber opera, through a ballet or modern dance studio to a number

Towers in use with retractable seating extended.

Studio stage with retractable seating extended.

of end stage, corner, thrust and transverse stage formats. Many of these were able to accommodate more than the nominal 200 audience members but after much deliberation a set of interesting layouts with approximately the right numbers were agreed. The room was also fitted with a number of acoustic panels, which could be raised and lowered, and some sound-absorbing curtains, mounted amongst the technology at high level, to allow for the different acoustic requirements.

Studio stage with seating retracted.

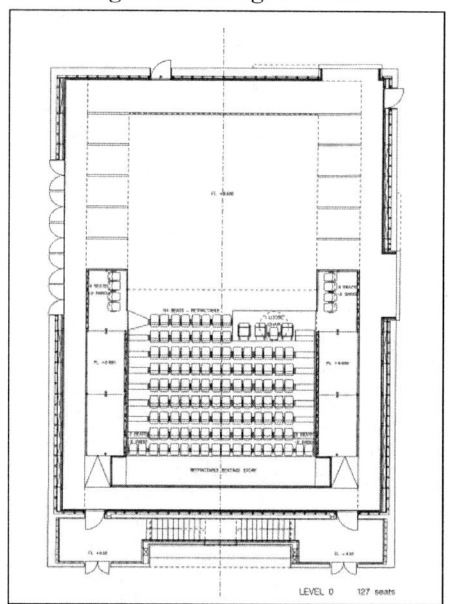
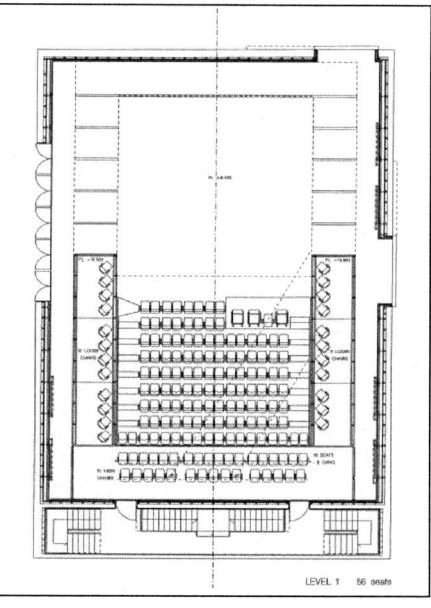

End stage plan with 9.9 nominal proscenium showing 3 wheelchair positions. Total 183-195 seats.

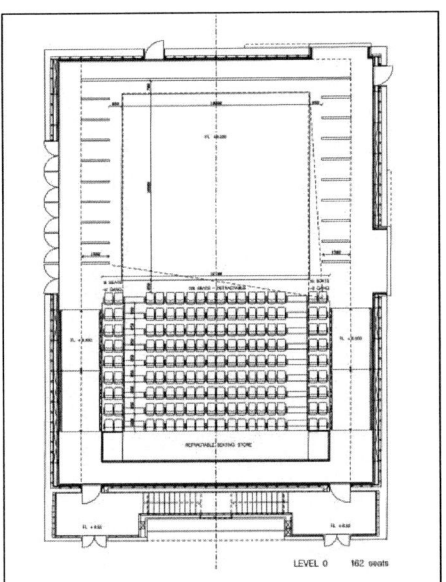
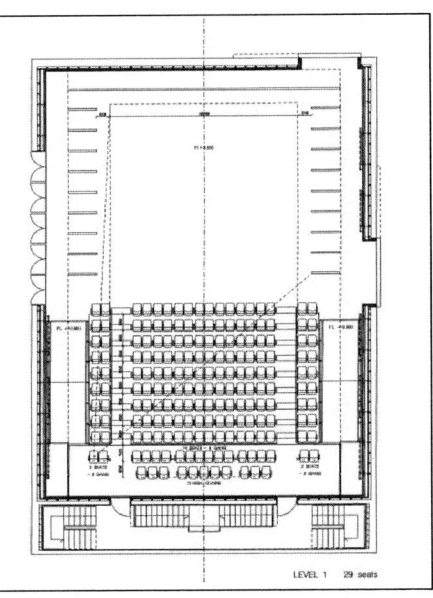

End stage plan with 11.3 m nominal proscenium for dance. Total 193 seats.

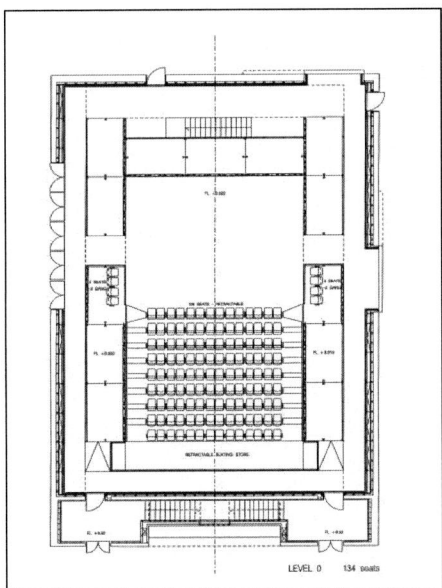
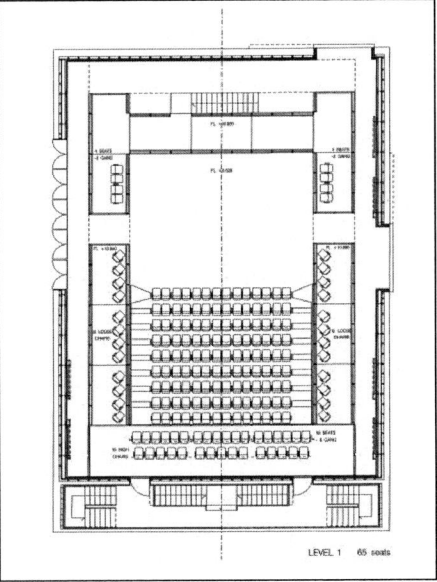

Recital or ensemble layout with 199 seats.

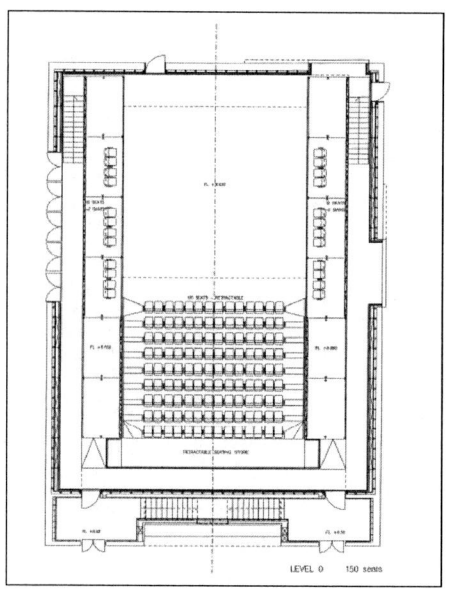
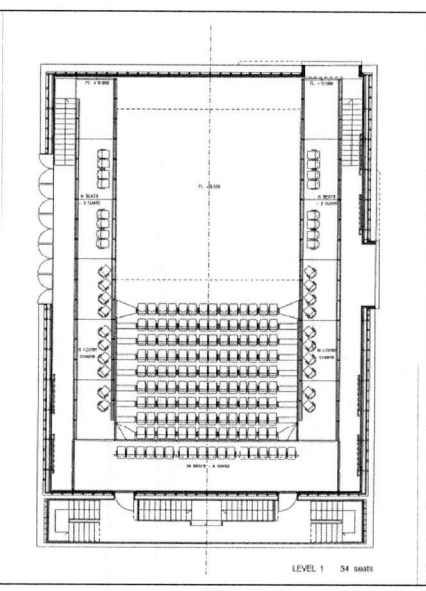

End stage with side galleries. Total 204 seats.

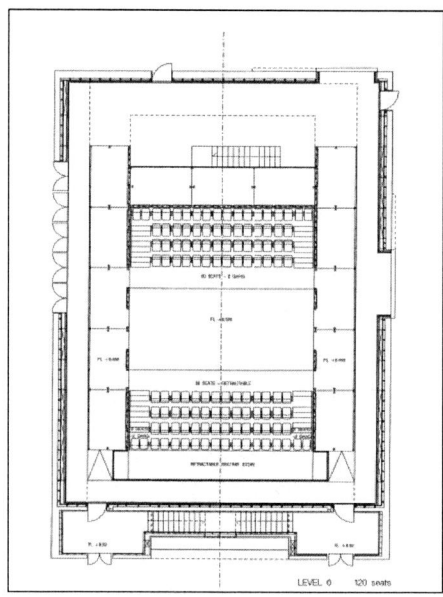
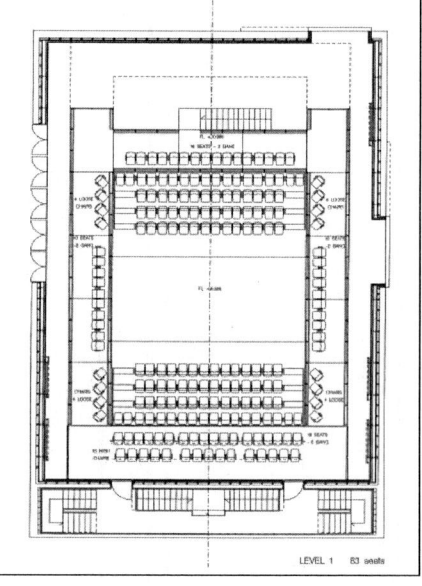

Small transverse stage with 205 seats.

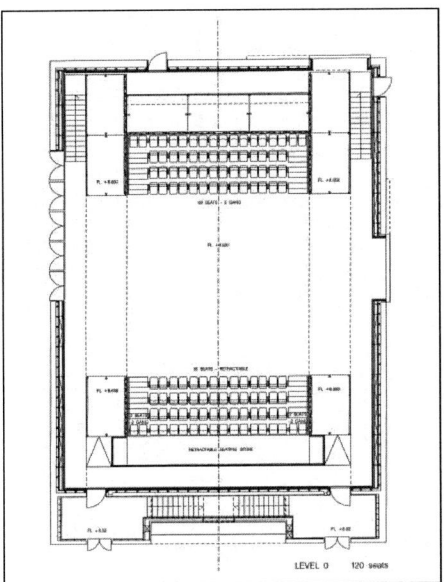
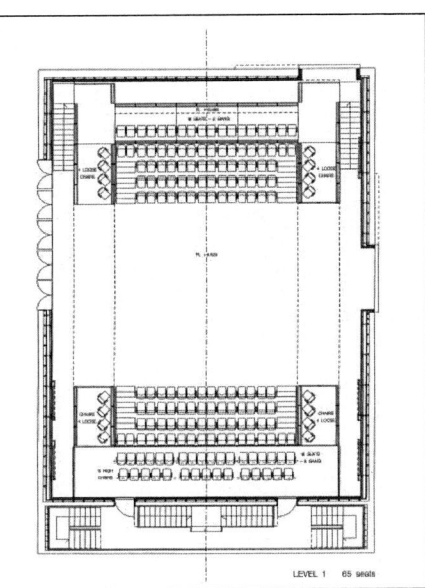

Wide transverse stage with 187 seats

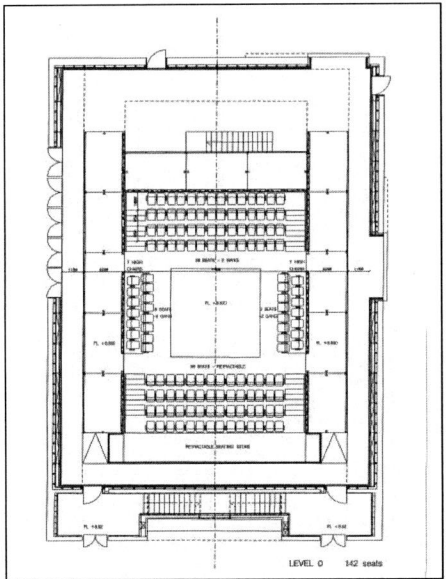
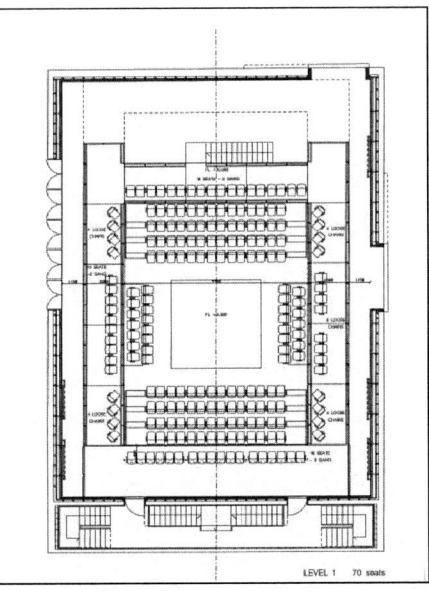

Theatre in the round with small stage and 212 seats.

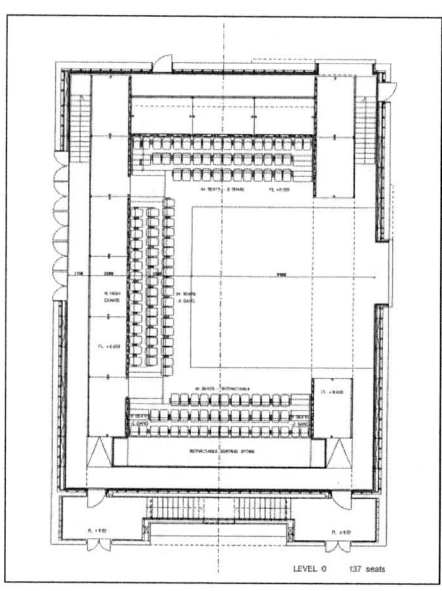
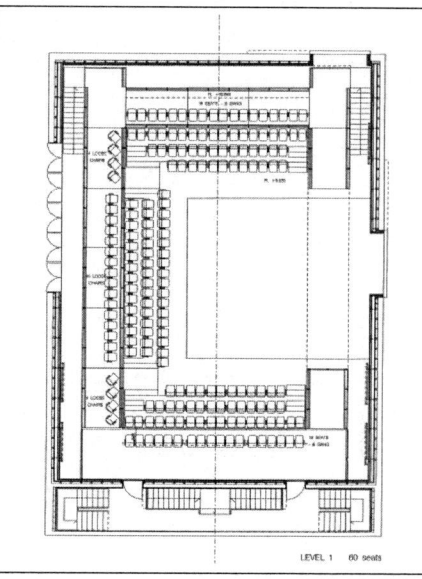

Side thrust stage format with 197 seats.

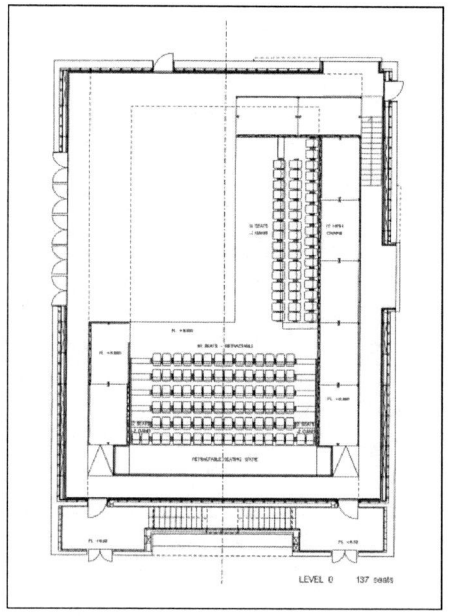
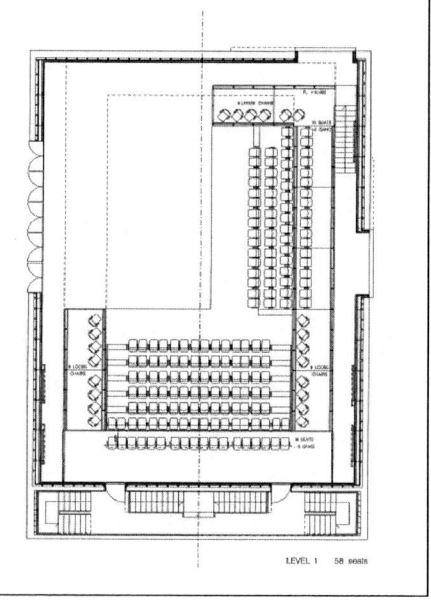

Corner stage with 195 seats.

66 Copenhagen Opera House

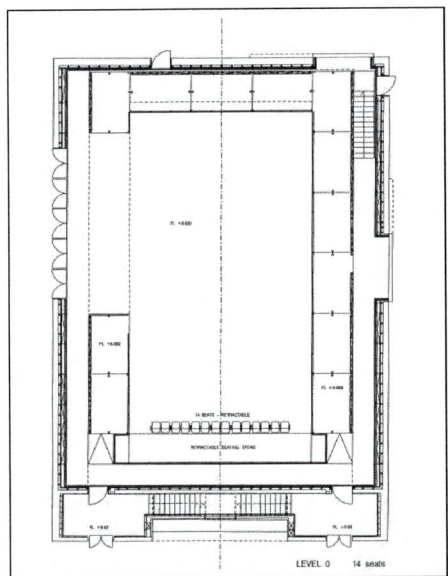 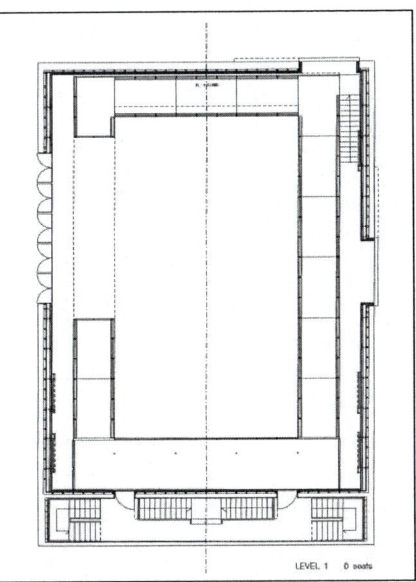

Daytime workshop with large windows exposed.

Dance rehearsal in the studio stage.

The various formats also required different escape arrangements and considerable flexibility in the moving balcony units. Separate stairways were included to allow exits from the top level of the moving balcony units when these did not align with the installed balcony. To achieve the required flexibility each of the moving balcony units was designed to be identical, with similar removable handrails and hinging acoustic panels at the back of the lower sections. This was planned so as to eliminate the need to place a particular moving balcony unit in any given position and limit the number of moves necessary in any changeover. Unfortunately this subtlety was missed when the project manager requested savings and so only a few towers were provided with the necessary adaptable fittings. This precluded creating some of the formats but again a compromise was reached and modifications were made to some further moving balcony units. Unfortunately this could not

Concrete access space at the side of the tensioned-wire grid area.

Gallery steelwork and hangers for tensioned-wire grid panels.

Locking device for tensioned-wire grid panels.

Tensioned-wire grid from below during construction.

extend to the internal wiring that had been designed to reduce the amount of cabling necessary to run to lighting and sound equipment which will be used on the towers.

Despite the reduction in overall height of the studio stage volume it did just prove possible to install a tensioned-wire grid with some multi-line hoists and chain hoists, along with production lighting facilities, above it. The grid is at 6.9 metres above stage floor and consists of a number of separate steel-framed panels with tensioned-wire grids in them. The panels were made in the Slingco factory in the UK and shipped out to be located on spigots installed on hangers attached to the overhead structure. This design expedites installation and also allows individual panels to be removed when required for a production, for example so that something can be flown higher than the grid or even for an entry to be made from overhead. There is a gap between each tensioned-wire grid panel so that the wire ropes from a number of multi-line hoists can drop through. These hoists are mounted on rolling beams and can therefore be moved up and down the studio within their bays to suit the rigging layout. These suspensions can be augmented by chain hoists which hang through the openings in the tensioned-wire grid itself. The chain hoists roll along beams which also roll across the studio in each bay, making for a great deal of adjustment of the rigging facilities. With the fly bars removed the attachments on the multi-line wire ropes and chain hoist hooks can be raised above the level of the grid to leave the studio clear.

The studio stage is intended to be used in a wide variety of ways but can be set up in a number of pre-determined forms in which it does not need further dressing or scenery. It has generally been kept a dark colour with black towers, dark grey seating and flooring. Attempts at completely hiding all the production lighting and sound services on the lower part of the walls were not fulfilled due to necessary economies but have probably made the studio easier to use. The limitations on space are not noticeable by the audience or on the stage floor but are

An audience arriving in the studio stage.

apparent to the technicians in the dimmer and sound rooms as well as in the grid space. There are no fixed control rooms as the flexibility of the space requires these positions to be set up on the technical gallery to suit the production or event. Cable ducts, openings and fixing points are provided to facilitate this in each of the many ways the studio can be used.

The Takelloftet, or 'rigging loft' as the studio stage is known, has been very popular with the Royal Theatre and has been used for a number of shows since the opening, including both ballet and opera.

Dance performance in the Takelloftet.

7 THE ACOUSTIC DESIGN OF OPERAEN
Jeremy Newton

Acoustic Design Principles and Room Geometry

Acoustic designers and noise control advisors Arup Acoustics worked alongside architects Henning Larsens Tegnestue (HLT), theatre planners Theatreplan and building services and structural engineers Rambøll to create a modern auditorium with a traditional horseshoe plan form to the balcony fronts. The numbers of seats in the stalls and each of the three audience tiers are as set out earlier in the description of the development. The architectural form of the auditorium was inspired by the desire to open the rear of the gently-sloping stalls onto the east-west axis across the water through Amalienborg Square which houses the Royal Palace, to the impressive dome of Frederik's Church. This resulted in a form with no stalls circle, lifting the balconies to create a 3m high wall around the stalls, as found in opera houses such as the Semperoper in Dresden, and more recently in Goteborgs Operan in Gothenburg. The room volume, including that above the technical gallery but excluding that above the convex ceiling, is around 10,500m^3, giving a total volume of around 7.1m^3/person.

The acoustic design for the room centred upon a providing adequate reverberance for the larger scale operas (Strauss, Wagner) whilst retaining excellent vocal intelligibility for the earlier Italian repertoire.

The stalls and three tiers of the auditorium.

The design target was to achieve an occupied mid-frequency reverberation time of 1.5 seconds, with an early decay time of 80 – 90% of this for sources on the stage and of 90 – 100% of this for sources in the orchestra pit.

The introduction of an architectural proscenium which was to be variable in width, such that a wide opening between stage and auditorium could be created if desired by the director, caused some difficulties. The widest to which this can be set is 17.4 metres, while a more normal setting is between 15 and 13.5 metres. The height of the architectural proscenium opening may be varied from 11 to 13.2 metres above stage level. The decision to allow for such wide settings pushed the proscenium walls, which are useful in providing supporting early-sound reflections to the stalls from the performers on stage, to 18.5 metres apart which is relatively wide for a room of around 1470 capacity. The maximum width at stalls level is 24 metres, while the outer walls at balcony level are 28 metres apart at the widest point. This dimension is reduced towards the stage by including additional sound reflecting surfaces downstage of the proscenium, which maintain the reflections of sound from

A view of the proscenium with the forestage elevator raised.

the stage into the main room volume as much as possible. The farthest seats in the stalls are 23.5 metres from the stage edge. The most distant seat in the third balcony is around 33 metres from the stage front.

Walls and Balcony Fronts

The auditorium outer walls are constructed from gypsum board (30 kg/m^2) with a massive inner lining of up to 75mm of stained maple. Into this timber lining are scribed 'L' shaped recesses developed by HLT and Arup Acoustics in an aesthetically sensitive response to the acoustic demands for high frequency sound scattering. The purpose of the scattering on the walls is to reduce acoustic 'glare'. The macro-shaping of the walls is designed to reflect the sound towards the middle and rear of the room. The wall geometry in the room is set out by identifying radial points from the centre point of a circle from which the curved plan form of the balcony fronts is also defined. The vertical section of each of the balcony fronts morphs from its most curved form at the rear of the auditorium to a more planar angled form close to the proscenium. This transition from angled to convex occurs so as to maximise the useful sound reflections from the angled part but also to ensure that the convex form is present to counteract the potential focusing effects of the circular plan geometry and to minimise strong high-frequency reflections from the sound system back to the stage or into the stalls.

The angled section of the balcony fronts is used to direct high-frequency sound from the stage to various seating areas. The first balcony front provides reflections to the stalls, the second balcony front to the second and third tiers. The third balcony front and technical gallery balcony fronts could not be angled to provide useful first reflections and are therefore gently sound scattering in nature. Although the balcony fronts are gently curved in vertical section, the solution to the architectural lighting in the space offered an opportunity to provide some high frequency scattering inspired by the plaster modelling on traditional balcony fronts. The continuously changing curvature of the balcony fronts was sculpted out of a solid timber laminate between 25mm and 75mm thick.

Between the balcony fronts and the outer wall of the auditorium is a further set of surfaces, the 'box fronts'. These were introduced as a means to provide the level changes and balustrades for the audience levels in the side balconies and, closer to the proscenium, were developed to give full height wall elements that reduce the acoustic width of the auditorium. The surfaces closest to the

The balcony fronts.

proscenium create a shallow balcony overhang, providing important early reflections and maintaining the propagation of sound into the main body of the room, as opposed to losing the lateral sound as one would with deeper balcony overhangs. These surfaces are constructed of 38mm timber on a steel frame and are textured with a reduced (in both size and depth) form of the high-frequency sound scattering 'L-shapes' found on the outer walls.

The soffits to the underside of the first, second and third tiers are constructed from 15mm thick 'Nesporex' panels, with a mass of $18kg/m^2$, that are bent across a framework of timber noggins with semi-random spacing to vary the resonant frequency of the construction and avoid excessive low frequency absorption. These panels are veneered to achieve the same aesthetic as the balcony fronts. The design philosophy for the room finishes was to provide sound scattering on necessary parts of the vertical planes, the walls, but to leave the horizontal surfaces generally smooth in nature. Some small grooves in the soffits provide very limited high frequency scattering. The front part of the soffits beneath the second and third tiers is more or less horizontal, to provide useful early reflection to the rows at the rear, and to encourage cue-ball reflections (sound reflections propagating off two adjacent perpendicular surfaces) at the sides closer to the proscenium. The soffit above the third tier (to the underside of the technical gallery and follow spot room) is constructed with a surface mass of $30kg/m^2$ and has been designed to provide mid- and high-frequency sound scattering in an aesthetically sensitive way. There are also some ventilation grilles in this ceiling that allow the build up of heat below to dissipate through the ceiling and be extracted above.

The fourth 'balcony front' in the room belongs to the technical gallery. It was considered important that this technical gallery did not significantly hinder the passage of sound into the upper reaches of the auditorium. Consequently the floor and rear balustrade have been made as acoustically transparent as possible. The floor is a metal grille, and the rear balustrade open with a very thin black fabric stretched across to minimise the view of the technology on the gallery from the third tier. Both surfaces have an architectural facing of timber slats.

Seating and Flooring

The seats were based on a custom design by the architects and were made by Race Seating UK Ltd. The seats are fully upholstered, with material on the back and to the underside of the squab. Some seats in the tiers where the rake is steeper have higher seat backs than elsewhere in the auditorium for safety reasons. The sound absorption of an array of 24 seats, including a number of high backed seats pro-rata to the numbers in the auditorium and both unoccupied and occupied, was measured in an acoustic laboratory.

Following the acoustic testing, initial concerns of under-absorption due to the slimness of the seat design were allayed and the absorption was found to be within the specified limits. The test results show only a small change between the absorption provided by the seating array in its unoccupied and occupied states.

This is borne out by measurements of the reverberation time in the auditorium. These show a desirably small mid-frequency reduction of just 0.18 secs between rehearsal and full audience conditions. The design target of restricting the change in reverberation time to 0.2 secs between unoccupied and occupied states has been achieved, allowing rehearsals to take place in a similar acoustic to that encountered during performances.

The stalls floor is constructed of timber over a ventilation plenum. The timber is approximately 65 mm thick (a composite of 15mm hardwood and 50 mm plywood).

The stalls seating.

Variable Acoustics

To reduce the reverberance in the room for an electronic repertoire and create conditions more suited to amplified sound, the auditorium is equipped with extensive areas of retractable sound absorbing banners that extend down the wall behind the seating in the second balcony and also from the third balcony upwards. In addition, manually-moveable sound-absorptive panels can be supported from grooves in the wall finish behind the seating in the first balcony. These panels enable the large areas of glass in the control room windows to be covered with sound absorption, if desired, to eliminate sound reflections from the loudspeakers back to the stage. Using these measures, the mid frequency reverberation may be reduced by up to 0.17 secs and late sound energy that may adversely affect the sound from loudspeakers may be controlled. Although this is quantitatively a similar reduction to that achieved when the seats are occupied, subjectively, adding the sound absorbing banners controls the late reverberance in the space, particularly that emanating from high level in the room, thus changing the perceived acoustic in the space.

The acoustic banners lowered.

The Orchestra Pit

The orchestra pit can be varied in height (vertically) and depth (horizontally) using three elevators. The elevator nearest the stage is 3.7 metres deep, the mid elevator is 2.7 metres deep and the furthest elevator from the stage only accommodates one row of seats and is 0.9 metres deep. The orchestra pit is on average 19m wide. The design of the orchestra pit was based on accommodating 104 musicians as required for *Electra* at an average spacing without using the overhangs. The largest possible orchestra pit playing area is 187m^2, which includes 51m^2 beneath overhangs at the stage front and at the sides of the pit. The area under the stage front overhang is 1.4 metres deep and this can be closed off with panels that track forward and backwards and which are acoustically variable. The panels comprise a metal frame with an inner panel that can be rotated to provide either a sound absorptive or sound reflective surface facing the orchestra pit. These can be used in absorptive mode to control the local reflections, from the horns for example, and in reflective mode to help project more sound out into the auditorium, as when set behind the basses. Further sliding panels can reduce the openings to the overhangs on either side of the pit.

The orchestra pit floor is constructed of plywood sheets pinned together to create 45mm thick timber plane in order to create the necessary acoustic conditions. This timber is supported over joists with semi-random spacing of between 450mm and 650mm. The pit is ventilated through purpose-made grilles set into the floor. The grilles can be rotated to provide a solid surface when the elevators are used as a forestage and also to allow the movement of the seating wagons on air castors. Fresh air is supplied to the void beneath the orchestra pit and allowed to seep through the grilles and other small openings in the floor, such as the cracks between the elevators.

The orchestra rehearsing in the large pit.

The orchestra pit rail has removable solid panels on the orchestra pit side that enable variation in its sound reflecting properties. The sections of the pit rail can hence be either sound reflecting or acoustically transparent. This variability may be used when the balance of different sections of the orchestra needs fine-tuning. For example, the acoustically transparent option may be utilised if a brighter string sound is desired in the stalls.

In order to facilitate the movement of large instruments between the orchestra pit and the orchestra rehearsal room in the basement, directly below the auditorium, there is a special lift for musical instruments on the stage left side of the orchestra pit. This expedites the frequent daily movement of instruments between these two important locations.

The Ceiling

Directly above the orchestra pit is a sound reflector with lighting slots in it. The purpose of this reflector is two-fold: partly to reflect sound from the orchestra back to the pit in order to help ensemble playing across the orchestra, and partly to provide early sound reflections from the stage to the stalls to support the direct sound and improve vocal clarity. The angle of this surface is close to horizontal to avoid directing too much orchestral sound into the stalls from overhead.

Above the main auditorium volume floats a fine gold-leaf ceiling. The gold ceiling is convex in both longitudinal and transverse section to spread sound reflections over a wider audience area. It is constructed of gypsum and plywood boards. It has a surface mass of $40kg/m^2$ to minimise low frequency sound absorption. Small grooves within the ceiling offer some surface modulation to reduce the potential for harshness of sound reflections. Within the ceiling are holes for theatrical lighting, offering an integrated solution that balances the requirements for the theatre lighting positions with the need for sound reflections from as much of the ceiling as possible. The aim was to minimise the open areas through which sound can be lost while still providing good ceiling lighting positions. Over each of the lighting holes is a sound-reflecting enclosure to further minimise sound loss into the void above the convex ceiling. The volume above the convex ceiling is cut off from the auditorium by a vertical upstand that extends up to 300mm from the soffit. This is not full height in order to allow air to be extracted from the ducts above the ceiling. This is again a compromise as acoustically it is more important to close off the volume above the convex ceiling than to allow sound to propagate above it. Around the edge of the convex ceiling is a lighting gallery that incorporates the follow spot room on the main axis

The ceiling and technical gallery towards the rear of the auditorium.

of the auditorium. The space around the convex ceiling provides substantial volume to assist the development of reverberance in the auditorium.

Roof Structure

The followspot room and technical gallery are hung from the cantilevered roof structure, and allowance for differential movement between this construction and the rest of the auditorium was made by movement joints that were engineered to provide a high degree of sound insulation between the foyer and the auditorium. Great attention was paid to the detailed construction around this movement joint, especially ensuring that there were no bridges across any gaps in the wall and floor constructions and finishes, to avoid noise in the auditorium from the differential movement generated by wind on the cantilever roof.

The Achievement

Measurement Analysis

Detailed room acoustic measurements were made in the unoccupied auditorium with the stage dressed for an opera production using a set from an earlier production of *Turandot* and a significant quantity of flown cloths. The mid-frequency reverberation time in the fly tower alone for the unoccupied measurements was similar to that in the auditorium, but it was somewhat longer at low frequencies. Measurements of the room acoustic (impulse responses) were also made with an audience present during an acoustic test performance. The average of mid frequency reverberation time ($T_{30,\,mf}$) measurements is 1.55 secs unoccupied, and 1.4 secs occupied. The average of T_{30} measurements in the 125Hz octave band is 1.95 secs unoccupied and 1.65 secs occupied.

Listening Analysis

The auditorium offers a well-balanced, warm, clear sound. The presence of the sound from the stage is very good, particularly towards the rear of the stalls and in the balconies. The pit sound is well blended in all but the first few rows of the stalls, and balances excellent musical clarity with adequate reverberance for most opera types. Tonally the sound is very beautiful, lacking in harshness and supported by a rich bass. The absence of noise (when not compromised by projection equipment or noisy lighting in the fly tower) provides the foundation for the conductor to exploit a great dynamic range.

Building Services

Noise from building services in the auditorium is inaudible. It was measured as perceived noise criterion (PNC) 6. The ventilation system uses low-velocity supply air fed through under-seat displacement grilles from air plena beneath the seats. The system was designed by Rambøll and acoustically engineered by Arup Acoustics. Extract is from high level above the convex ceiling and through holes in the walls at the back of each balcony.

The ventilation system is designed to operate using the displacement philosophy. The air is supplied into under-floor supply plenums and enters the auditorium through terminal units located in the floor either beneath the seats in the stalls and some locations in the tiers, or behind the seats in the vertical risers in parts of the tiers. The air is extracted through openings with no grilles at the rear of the stalls and each balcony overhang, and from the top of the room above the convex ceiling. The main auditorium air handling units are located behind the fly tower and the ductwork passes through the motor room above the grid and down the face of the fly tower before distributing in the zone between the upper concrete slab that encloses the auditorium and the cantilevered roof structure. From this location the ducts drop down risers to feed the plenums on each level. Air is supplied at a rate of between 11 and 12 litres per second per person. The under-seat displacement units were developed for the project by Lindab and tested in the laboratory to ensure that they would meet the exacting demands for low noise generation. The achievement of imperceptible noise from the building services in the auditorium creates the best possible dynamic range in which to express the music. The down side to this silence is that any noise from any source in the stage or fly tower is more obvious, and potentially disturbing.

Sound Insulation

Low noise levels demand a high standard of sound insulation to ensure that there is no disturbance from nearby noisy activities. This is achieved all around the auditorium by virtue of sound absorbing lobbies and circulation spaces that wrap around the auditorium between it and the foyer. The sound insulation is maintained through the large opening at the rear of the stalls by three sets of sound-reducing hinged doors and a pair of sliding doors. In order to break up the sound-focusing potential of the natural form of the hinged doors, they are clad with timber providing convex curvature and are modulated in the same way as the walls of the auditorium to provide high frequency sound scattering. Sound insulation between the auditorium and the orchestra rehearsal room below is of a very high standard, achieving in excess of 60dB at low frequencies.

House Lighting

The house lighting was designed by Speirs and Major Associates and engineered by Rambøll. After discussions with Arups, it utilises low-noise LED sources in the balcony fronts and fibre-optic sources for the balconies. The fibre-optic sources are mainly located outside the auditorium volume to eliminate any noise from cooling fans in the fibre-optic engines. Special fanless engines (with glass optical cables) are situated in the technical balcony and above the convex ceiling where harness lengths precluded external engine locations. The central stalls area is lit by ETC Source 4 luminaires located in the openings in the convex ceiling and other fittings on the technical balcony provide other feature lighting. The full house lighting scheme is described in Chapter 12.

Sound System

The house sound system consists of a central cluster located above the proscenium opening, an array of loudspeakers either side of the proscenium (one at each level of the auditorium) and fill loudspeakers situated in the stage-front, supported by two sub-woofers located at either side on the over-pit acoustic reflector. There is also a distributed array of loudspeakers for sound effects that have been integrated into the room architecture. This is more fully described in Chapter 13.

Ancillary Rooms

There are two rooms, one either side of the rear entrance to the stalls, which can be used as producer's rooms, for surtitle control, audio description or commentaries. The glass on the auditorium side of the two-layer sound insulating window separating these rooms from the auditorium is angled to avoid adverse sound reflections. In addition to these spaces, there are three technical control rooms at the rear of the first tier for lighting, scenery projection and sound. All these rooms also have a high degree of sound insulation from the auditorium. Only the sound control room has an openable window which uses a custom-made design by Theatreplan. A sheet of glass slides vertically by the action of a small winch and is sealed when in its raised position by pneumatic seals all round its periphery to give the required sound insulation. The sound absorbing room finishes to the walls and ceiling and anti-static carpet on the floor within these rooms ensures a suitably controlled acoustic environment.

The Theatre Equipment

The sound-reducing properties of the large dividing doors between the main stage and the various side stages were determined by Arup and provided to Theatreplan for incorporation in the Employer's Requirements. So that works can continue on stage during rehearsals in the orchestra pit, the fire curtain that separates the auditorium from the main stage had to achieve a sound reduction of 45dB. The three huge sound-reducing fire-rated shutters that acoustically separate the main stage from the rear stage and from side stage left and side stage right also achieve 45dB, enabling work to continue in the side and rear stages during a rehearsal or performance on the main stage.

The rehearsal stage is separated from the rear stage by two 11.2 metre high sets of manually-operated panel doors, spaced from each other by 1.5 metre.

The view from side stage right across the mainstage to the rehearsal stage.

Each of these panel doors is rated at $R_w = 51$dB when closed. Careful detailing, especially of the sound-reduction panels installed under the compensating elevators that are beneath these doors, and a high-quality of installation have resulted in an overall sound reduction between the rear stage and the rehearsal stage of 63dB. This degree of separation enables noisy set building works to be carried out in the rear stage without disturbing rehearsals in the rehearsal stage. The side and rear stages all have sound absorption pin-fixed to the concrete soffits to help control noise build-up. The rehearsal stage acoustic also benefits from sound absorption on two adjacent walls, located horizontally between 'shelves' that may be used for resting scenery against. The bottom 2 metres of these walls is sound reflecting, but have angled surfaces in between the shelves to avoid flutter echoes.

The specifications for the stage elevators, flying system, stage wagons and both equaliser and compensator elevators around the stage, the dividing door hoists, house curtain mechanisms and stage lighting all included stringent requirements for the control of noise. The development of this equipment is described in more detail in Chapter 9.

*The set for **Aida** being moved on stage on the stage wagons.*

A significant effort was been made by all parties to ensure that the noise from the theatre equipment is not intrusive during quiet moments in performances.

The motors for the stage elevators were installed upon massive vibration-isolating concrete inertia bases and, along with the control cabinets, were enclosed in a room three floors below the stage. This has resulted in the stage elevators being some of the most silent in the world, achieving 25 dBL$_{Aeq}$ at the head of the conductor when they are being raised or lowered.

The system of stage wagons used to transport sets or elements of sets between the six stages are also surprisingly quiet. The wagons move on special triple-swivel castors and are driven by toothed pinion wheels that rise through openings in the stage floor on which the wagons move. While basic noise reduction steps were taken in design and fabrication there were not many choices available but accurate fabrication and careful installation appears to have paid off. The equaliser and compensator elevators, most of which are fortunately outside the main stage area and which are not often operated during a performance are not as quiet as specified, largely due to screw-jack drives which are difficult to silence and in some places inadequate isolation of the mechanisms from the building.

The power flying system is also silent, measuring 26dBL$_{Aeq}$ at the head of the conductor with four bars operating simultaneously. The only audible noise source from the flying system is the ropes passing over the pulleys up at high-level in the grid. With other items also achieving near-enough their noise specification, the theatre machinery installation can maintain the magical illusion of noiseless movement.

Orchestra Rehearsal Room

The orchestral rehearsal room, which measures 21.5 x 19.8 metres in plan and 10.1 metres high, is located 12 metres below water level, directly beneath the auditorium. In order to reduce noise from passing ships and to provide maximum sound insulation between it and the auditorium, this Rehearsal Room was constructed as an acoustically isolated 'box-in-box' construction. Pre-cast concrete wall and floor elements are supported by pads of an elastomeric material, 'Sylomer', to give the structure a natural frequency of around 12Hz. On the walls and the ceiling there is a carefully designed array of tuned low frequency sound absorbers, convex sound scattering devices, broadband sound absorption and vertically moving sound absorbing panels that can be

The orchestra rehearsal room.

used to make the room acoustic more critical and to tune the space to give a similar room response for different ensemble sizes. The vertical panels are moved using a simple rotating spindle system. The reverberation time in the unoccupied room is flat across the frequency bands, giving a slight low frequency rise of 10% when occupied. The movable panels allow variation of the mid frequency reverberation time from 1.4 to 1.1 seconds and have four pre-set configurations controlled from a wall mounted panel located by the main entrance. The complex system of acoustic components on the walls and ceiling is visually screened by a wall lining of slotted medium density fibreboard panels and feature a wavy ceiling created from timber strips, creating a fine working space for the orchestra and choir.

Very low noise levels (PNC12) from ventilation via 'jet' nozzles and silent light sources, coupled with the high degree of sound insulation from adjacent spaces make the room highly suitable for recording as well as rehearsal. Separated from the rehearsal room by deep-cavity double glazing is a control room that may be used for recording and monitoring without noise intrusion from the rehearsal room or from the surrounding musician's lounge.

Takelloftet

Also constructed as an isolated 'box-in-box' is the Takelloftet, or studio stage, which is located on the first floor in the north-east corner of the building. This construction is necessary to control the noise from the nearby scenery lift, deliveries to the load-in docks and a trash compactor in the area beneath. The interior of this studio stage measures 22.7 x 16.6 metres in plan and it is designed as a flexible space to accommodate a variety of performances from chamber music to recitals, small scale opera, dance, amplified events and jazz. The overall height of the room at 9.7 metres provides adequate acoustic volume for musical use, although as noted elsewhere the height of the room does restrict the technical space. The tensioned-wire grid is located at a height of 6.9 metres above the floor level. The space can be configured to accommodate various theatrical functions using both retractable and loose seating and a number of moving balcony 'tower' units. This is described more fully in Chapter 6.

The Studio Stage showing the tensioned-wire grid.

At the side of the room but within its volume and above the tensioned-wire grid are located the air supply and extract ducts. Jet nozzles were once again the chosen solution, silently blowing air across the space and down the long sidewalls. Acoustically, the lower part of the outer walls are faced with angled panels to avoid flutter echoes when opposite walls are exposed, for example when the room is being used in the flat floor configuration with none of the moving balcony units in use. The movable balcony units can be used either to provide balconies for audience seating or can be rotated to provide a sound reflecting surface around the stage for chamber music recitals and similar musical events. The vertical surfaces of the movable balcony units are also angled to provide some sound scattering. Some of these are also hinged to provide access through the units at low level.

To complement the flexibility of the space there are also some variable acoustics. These comprise of two elements: theatrical black wool serge curtains above the tensioned wire grid on each side of the room that may be extended the full length of the space, and material-clad mineral fibre panels that can be lowered down the walls from storage enclosures at high level. The resulting variation of mid-frequency reverberation time in the unoccupied space as set up for chamber music performances is between 1.7 and 1.3 seconds.

Foyer

The foyer wraps around the auditorium shell and offers five floors of dramatic, light, airy, spacious circulation and entertainment space. The acoustic environment is controlled by perforated metal ceilings at every level and a perforated metal lining to the roof lights that bathe the auditorium shell with daylight. The result is a lively but well controlled acoustic, well suited to socialising. The mid-frequency reverberation time in the space is controlled to 1.3 secs.

Recording Studio

Beneath side stage right is the sound suite which includes a recording studio and a recording control room. The recording studio is constructed as a plasterboard box-in-box sitting on an isolated concrete slab. A sound reduction between the rooms of 65dB has been achieved. The window separating the two rooms has an angled pane on the control room side to avoid strong horizontal reflections across the room. The room's acoustics are deadened through incorporation of a perforated plasterboard

The foyers at night.

finish, carpet on the floor and a sound absorbing perforated metal ceiling. The room response is well controlled throughout the 100Hz – 5kHz range. Impacts on the stage are inaudible in the recording room, despite a very low background noise level (PNC 13).

Opera, Ballet, Music Practice and Chorus Rehearsal Rooms

Above the side stages around the fly tower are two floors of rehearsal rooms. Many of the rehearsal rooms are constructed as a plasterboard 'room within a room' on an isolated concrete slab to minimise noise disturbance from adjacent spaces. There is a dedicated chorus rehearsal room, two ballet studios, an opera rehearsal room and numerous instrumental practice and vocal coaching rooms of different sizes. The slatted architectural finish to the walls and ceiling hides the sound absorption and services installations, and sound scattering walls (to reduce flutter echoes) are expressed in a zigzag form. Structurally isolated double-glazing helps to maintain the sound insulation from occupational noise within the building. The high quality craft traditions of Denmark have enabled unusually high standards of sound insulation to be achieved throughout the Opera, and these enable parallel activities without mutual disturbance. Noise from building services, using chilled ceilings in the small rooms and jet nozzles in the large, is well controlled to around NR 20 in each space.

Throughout the building the complex acoustic requirements have been rationally integrated into the design in a way that makes the acoustic elements appear to be intrinsic to the room architecture. The result is a technically demanding but beautiful building that is crafted to provide world-class facilities of the highest acoustic standards.

A typical rehearsal room.

8 CONSTRUCTION AND EQUIPPING OF OPERAEN Richard Brett

Planning

Theatreplan had no direct involvement in the construction of the building structure but took a huge interest in the process in order to ensure that lessons learned on previous performing arts construction projects could be taken into account by the project management and construction team. The architects and engineers examined very early in the process whether a steel frame, in-situ or pre-cast concrete should be the preferred form of construction. Clearly, both the cost and the resources that would be available in Copenhagen during the next three and a half years had to be taken into account. The Client's project manager, Peter Poulsen, was also very interested in learning how other modern theatre buildings had been constructed.

My experience on projects ranging from the reinforced concrete of the National Theatre and Barbican in London, through projects in the UK and overseas, to the steel-framed fly towers of both the Gran Teatre del Liceu in Barcelona and the Royal Opera House in London, indicated a strong preference for in-situ concrete for the stage, side stages and fly tower. There are many load-bearing fixings required for equipment in these areas, and often other mountings for equipment are needed later after the project is handed over. To make these positively in a steel frame, particularly when heavily clad to ensure a good level of sound insulation, is difficult to achieve. Concrete is also beneficial in terms of sound insulation and the mass is very important in minimising equipment noise.

Copenhagen Opera in fact employed all three forms of construction. The deep basements, stage, side stages, fly tower and bulk of the building over the stage and side stages is built in on-site cast concrete, while parts of the rear of the building use pre-cast panels. This enabled the offices, dressing rooms and wardrobe accommodation to be constructed very rapidly once the ground floor slab was cast. The main mechanical plant and electrical intake and switchgear were placed under the ground floor with access for replacement through panels at the rear of the building. Other mechanical plant is located at a higher level over the rear stage at the back of the fly tower.

Sequencing

The sequencing of a major theatre building is also important. Knowing the time that it was likely to take to co-ordinate and install all the theatre technical and stage engineering equipment, Theatreplan proposed that the fly tower be constructed first. While the dimensions of this are critical and the spaces to accommodate not only the equipment but to ensure that the stage area will work properly have to determined in detail, these are faster to confirm and get drawn than the complex geometry of the auditorium. In fact the complexity of the auditorium, both the internal levels of the tiers and their form, and the curvature of the envelope appearing in the foyers, did not lend itself to concrete and was constructed in steel. This separation of disciplines actually worked well and probably allowed the best construction processes in each zone. Work on the stage areas and fly tower was given initial priority on site.

The Site

The site of the Opera was originally a naval dockyard and had to be cleared of old buildings and other debris. Because of its location in the harbour the water table was extremely high and the building had to be designed to be

Start on site in May 2002.

Shell of the Orchestra Rehearsal Room constructed at the lowest level.

The precast units used to construct the backstage offices

restrained using ground anchors to prevent it rising out of the ground during construction. When fully constructed the mass of the building reduces the need for the anchors. During the excavation for the orchestra rehearsal room and stage basement, the deepest parts of the site, old shipping wrecks were discovered. These turned out to be three Pomeranian merchant vessels, most likely sunk in the early 1400s when the Danes defended the port of Copenhagen against Hanseatic merchants. The potential delay of an archaelogical survey immediately set alarm bells ringing but the Client team ensured that the site investigations were carried out quickly and that concrete could continue to be poured. At one stage trucks were removing excavated material and others were arriving with concrete for other parts of the site in an almost continuous stream.

The orchestra rehearsal room under the main auditorium was to be a 'box within a box' in order to ensure the low background noise level required.

A tidy site - understage dimmer space!

Stage left of orchestra pit.

Orchestra pit showing seating stores below construction platform.

Clive Odom in the foreground inspects the site with Tyge Bruun from AP Møller.

Rehearsal room area on fourth floor with floating floor slab.

Special rubber pads on which the internal room is constructed were placed on piers on the basement slab. Considerable care was taken by the contractors, E. Pihl and Søn, to ensure the water-tightness of all the concrete construction below ground. One of the most noticeable features of the whole site was the organisation and tidiness which was apparent right from the start, wherever one went. While site gear was mandatory, the site was extremely safe, very good access was provided to wherever one needed to get and the usual dangers of materials discarded everywhere, as often seen on other European building sites, were virtually absent.

The Fly Tower

The fly tower has a stage basement 13 metres deep and a grid at 30 metres above the stage, plus a 4 metre high grid with a hoist motor room, dimmer room and air-duct space above it. To provide stability and services routes outside the working spaces on the

Service cores in construction.

The rear fly tower wall and service cores were constructed first.

Slip-form continuous-pour construction of the fly tower.

Temporary supports during slip-form construction of the fly tower.

Copenhagen Opera House 93

Cutting away the concrete supports in a side stage opening.

Night work on site.

galleries within the fly tower, two service towers were designed, one on each side at the rear of the tower. Each tower incorporates a builders work staircase from understage to the motor room and roof, serving each gallery and the grid, and linking to the rehearsal room and other accommodation built above the side and rear stages. The tower on the north (stage right) has a 6-person lift which also serves every level, (an essential feature for working the theatre) which was also made available to the installation crews. It is clear that this not only expedited the work but provided facilities for getting moderately-sized pieces of equipment up to levels once the site crane was removed and the external walls were completed.

The fly tower was poured using slip-form shuttering over a period of five to six weeks working round the clock. The site really looked impressive at this time and the fly tower was constructed virtually between two site visits by the Theatreplan team who were, at that time, travelling to the site only

Repertoire store with ballet wagon slot.

Structure for mainstage elevator guides.

Steel trusses for grid and gallery hangers in position.

Fly tower construction ready for steel roof trusses.

every month or so. At the lower level, the 11.2 metre high openings to the auditorium, side and rear stages were supported by concrete columns which were then cut away once the concrete walls above had cured and strengthened. There were other special 'theatrical' constructions required; one was the 17 metre long by 1 metre high slot at the rear of the stage basement through which the ballet wagon moves when it is taken out or returned to its store. This was also built as separate openings and made into one slot after the concrete had cured. The rear stage is a 300mm thick slab supported over a clear span of 22 metres by concrete beams 1.6 metres deep at 3 metre centres so that the ballet wagon can store beneath it. The work on the steelwork for the supports for the mainstage elevators and their counterweights commenced as soon as the stage basement was dry as these were the installations with the longest delivery and commissioning periods.

With the fly tower concrete complete, the huge steel trusses that support the loads in the fly tower and take them back to the downstage and upstage walls were erected. Theatreplan had insisted that these beams run in the up-down stage direction and that they were positioned so as to carry the diverter pulleys for the flying system and the hangers for the grid. Two other trusses support the hangers for the two side galleries. The space at each side of the grid was also made in concrete to provide a solid base for diverter pulleys for the dividing doors and a space on which small works could be carried out

Grid fitted and boarded over, and concrete gallery seen from below.

Grid boarded over before motor room slab poured.

Motor room structure and concrete floor.

Power flying drop pulleys fitted at high level in grid.

Power flying head pulleys fitted above hoists in motor room.

Motor room floor showing wire-rope holes with mountings for noise absorbers.

Power flying busbar tap-off points with individual hoist drive cabinets below.

Grid covered and with power flying wire ropes in coils.

without risk to those below. We also wanted a concrete gallery on which to mount the dividing door machinery; this wasn't required for fly tower stability on this project but an internal concrete gallery can sometimes be useful in this respect. This gallery is at 24.3 metres above the stage. The other galleries are in steel with timber flooring.

The grid decking was fitted and boarded over before the floor to the motor room above was poured.

This floor had to have openings for the wire ropes for the flying system every 400 mm in lines each side. We originally envisaged that these would be formed in the concrete but the contractor preferred to cast a complete slab on the profiled-steel sheet and to drill the holes afterwards with a diamond cutter. The finished result is satisfactory but the torn steel sheet on the underside was not particularly attractive! In the motor room the

Power flying wire ropes hanging at stage level.

Power flying grid head pulleys and slack-wire detection.

Copenhagen Opera House 97

holes are masked by acoustic absorbers. The hoists are mounted in cast-in channels in the motor room floor and the head and diverter pulley assemblies are fixed to secondary steelwork at high level. The power busbar system and individual electrical drives for the hoists are similarly mounted from the steelwork above.

The power flying installation was relatively fast in that there was little steel construction to be undertaken and the components, hoists, pulley assemblies, drive cabinets, wire ropes and similar were delivered to site and, with everything pre-planned, fitted quickly. The grid decking was covered with plywood as soon as it was installed which allowed the fitting of diverter pulleys in the grid area to be carried out safely whilst the elevators were being installed. The wire ropes were then lowered carefully in coils so as not to snag and as soon as a working floor could be fitted to the elevators, the flying bars were hung. These were finally levelled to the finished stage floor later. The only element of difficulty with the flying system was ensuring

The grid remained floored during testing of point hoists.

The completed grid area.

A multitude of flying bars.

The fly tower ready for external cladding.

the reliability of slack wire detection occurring independently on each of the seven suspension wire ropes. This is one of the most difficult parts of a modern power flying installation to achieve easily and reliably. More detail of the stage engineering and other technical installations is given in the following chapters.

The point hoists were installed in the motor room and the wire ropes reeved through to the diverter pulleys in the grid but the accuracy of the rolling beam positioning and the point hoist drops through the grille decking could not be determined until the temporary flooring over the grid was removed.

As often happens on a building site, 'services anarchy' ruled, although to a lesser extent than on many projects. Unfortunately sprinkler and other pipework installers often get to the site before the stage engineering contractor is ready to start and pipes are positioned where easiest, rather than to a co-ordinated drawing. However, the sense of responsibility over doing a good job on this project meant that, where there were good arguments for having work corrected, the project manager and main contractor instructed that items must be dismantled and installed correctly.

The Stage Floor Installations

The installation of mainstage elevators needs to be achieved quickly so that some form of working floor can be provided in the area for other trades as soon as possible. However, even when these large structures and their counterweights are in position there is a tremendous amount of further work to be completed. As soon as the wire rope suspensions for each elevator and the electric hoists are installed, there is a need to check the operation and

Mainstage elevator guides, pulleys and wire-ropes.

Mainstage elevator hoist installation before construction of noise enclosure.

Downstage elevator framework raised showing lower platform.

All four mainstage elevator frames at different levels.

Mainstage elevators with test weights on lower platform.

The completed upstage elevator fully raised.

Access equipment in rear and side stages.

Work on the equalisers in the rear stage.

View through equaliser platform structure showing screw-jack drives.

View under an equaliser elevator showing screw-jack drives and a wagon drive unit.

Equaliser elevator wedge and roller mechanism.

Three completed equalisers (one lowered) and a finished wagon.

alignment of the elevators frequently as other parts are fitted. Considerable planning was therefore required to allow other activities, such as the hanging of the fly tower galleries and installation of the large dividing doors to the side and rear stages and the safety curtain, to be carried out in parallel with the completion of the elevators.

It was clear from the prototype tests on the stage wagon and equaliser elevator equipment in the UK that considerable time had to be allowed for their installation and commissioning on site. Periods were allowed in the programme for the installation of the 25 full-size equaliser and compensator elevators and one half-size equaliser adjacent to the cloth store elevator. These form the majority of the floor surface throughout the side and rear stages and rehearsal stage, and their installation was to be followed by periods for the installation of the wagon drive units and commissioning of the stage wagons. The setting out needed to be accomplished with millimetre accuracy over an area of 44 metres by 64 metres on a building site with many other trades having

A stage wagon drive unit being lowered into place.

Adjusting a drive unit to ensure pinion alignment.

Rear and rehearsal stages showing wagon drive unit positions.

to pass through the designated area and sometimes having to work there as well. As many as eleven powered scissor lifts were counted in use in this area at one time!

Although the equaliser and compensator elevators had been envisaged as sectionalised and prefabricated units which could be easily assembled and set up on site, they came to site in smaller parts and required significant assembly work and time to get them completed. They also all had to be floored and edged accurately so that they were all level with each other when lowered, and with the wagons when raised. While the flooring on the stage wagons is pine panels painted black, that on the equalisers and compensator elevators is plywood covered with 9 mm oil-bound hardboard left unpainted. This difference indicates clearly which flooring will move vertically and which horizontally! The wagons and mainstage elevators have black ultra-high molecular polyethylene (UMHWPE) edging and the equalisers and compensators have white, again as a safety feature. This all had to be fitted securely within very tight tolerances.

As the structure of each elevator was finished, the stage wagon drive units were fitted and positioned accurately within them, ready to carry out tests on the wagon movements. While individual wagon movements in a rear or side stage could be checked, the overall setting out of the system was really only able to be tested when the software bugs in the system were eliminated and groups of wagons could move over the 64 metres across stage and 44 metres up and down stage. Although completion of this aspect of the work was on a knife-edge and the delays did cause significant concern to ourselves, the client and the project manager, the final performance of the wagon system is remarkable. It called to mind the observation made some 25 years previously by John Bury, then Head of Design at the National Theatre in London, after months of construction delays, about the computerised point hoist flying system in the Olivier Theatre, "The movement is superb and has been well worth waiting for!"

Steelwork frames for the main auditorium.

The Auditorium

The design of the steelwork for the auditorium by engineers Rambøll AS is a work of art in itself. The fabrication of this steelwork had to be started before the details of the levels and sightlines could be completed, but despite this there were only a couple of areas where the steel compromised what we would have liked to do on the tiers. The main pressures on the design from the theatre planning point of view were to establish the spacing of the tiers and the detail of the front row and balcony, where it is essential to minimise the structural thickness. Thickness in the floor structure at the

The first frames are positioned.

The completed auditorium envelope.

Copenhagen Opera House 103

The auditorium tier steelwork.

Auditorium tiers.

The minimal structure of the tier fronts.

Steel for auditorium side tiers being fitted.

front of the balcony lifts each tier and also thickens the effective depth of the balcony. It is important for this to be reduced by clever structural engineering as far as possible in the interests of the room design. After many discussions and examination of alternatives, the zone was minimised to an extent that made getting all the services through it difficult. Clearly we had achieved the main aim!

The steel frames were delivered to site and assembled into the envelope of the 'conch'. This immediately began to demonstrate just how close to the stage the tiers felt, an important assurance which comes from experience of many early visits to theatre construction sites! As soon as the balconies are formed, even if they are not clad and one is standing on builders' boards, it is often possible to tell whether the auditorium has the right 'feel' – whether it has the potential to be a great room with good contact with the stage. Copenhagen was one of those with a really positive feel and as the flooring progressed, the balcony and box fronts were constructed and the wall cladding was fixed, this feel became even more apparent.

The auditorium envelope seen through the proscenium.

The structure of the rear tiers was filled with reinforcement and concrete to form a basis for the timber construction of the seating rows and slip boxes. The space under the stalls and each of the tiers is a supply air plenum, with the extract above the convex ceiling. The tiers have air grilles in the risers while the air enters the stalls through horizontal grilles between the seats which are integrated into the seat base fixing. This particular seat design, with its base fixed in position before the seat itself, meant that any errors in placing the seats would only become apparent later. While there were minor positioning discrepancies which were corrected, the seats dropped into place beautifully, completing the image of a rich, intimate auditorium. In some of the special boxes in the side tiers the sightlines appeared better than anticipated and the unusual mounting of the front seats in the side tiers, one behind the other and close to the rail, paid off in much improved sightlines and seating comfort. Even the few seats provided with slightly higher seats and footrests adjacent to the side aisles in the upper tiers to ensure the best sightlines worked well and have been accepted by audiences.

The sections of the balcony front were manufactured off-site to very detailed dimensions defining the curve and form required for the required acoustic reflections. When the first sections were delivered to site it was found that the problem of tolerances had arisen and it was necessary to reduce the overall length of most sections to enable them to fit accurately. It is a great compliment to the Danish timber

Trial erection of a balcony front unit.

The first tier of the completed auditorium.

contractor Jakon A/S that the balcony fronts, the curved soffits and panelling on the conch in the foyers all fitted so beautifully.

The Foyers

The foyers in use.

The completed plaza level foyer with the Operaen symbol.

The multi-level foyers surround the 'conch' and are accessed by gentle staircases and glass lifts near the cloakrooms which are located nearest to the stage on each side. Audience toilets are provided at each level and downstairs

beneath the main ground floor foyer area. From the ground floor the audience can move into the rear of the stalls through large curved motorised doors that move sideways to reveal the steps up into the auditorium. Other motorised hinged doors at the rear of the stalls work with the sliding door to form the necessary light and sound lobby between the auditorium and foyer. On each upper level the audience can move into the auditorium across bridges and through doors in the conch shell. Construction of the foyer levels and bridges was again in steel with marble flooring. The curved façade was also steel construction.

Despite there being a number of difficulties to be overcome in fitting out the auditorium, with the finishes in the foyer, with the services and plant, as well as with the theatre installations and stage engineering, the project was managed in such a way that these were generally addressed in a constructive manner and resolved quickly. This is demonstrated by the fact that the building was completed on time and, although we did not agree with every decision made by the project managers, it was good to feel that one's arguments were being weighed against the benefit to the project rather than solely to get the work completed in the shortest time and with no extra expense. The result is there to be seen. A high-quality project.

9
STAGE ENGINEERING IN OPERAEN
Richard Brett, Clive Odom, Dave Ludlam

The cost of stage engineering installations in normal theatres often surprises even those in the construction industry – and it amazes those who have little concept of how such equipment has to perform and what it has to handle. When it comes to an opera house, the consultant is often just not believed and, as implied earlier, it takes a lot of hard work to demonstrate the reality of the situation.

The challenge that was presented to Theatreplan was to design a stage and fly tower, with the necessary understage and supporting side and rear stage areas that would enable the users to present three or four major operas in repertoire, together with ballet performances. The stage should be available for full scenic rehearsals during the day and there should be at least one major opera rehearsal space that could also accommodate scenery.

Stage Planning
This is not an unusual brief for a major opera house but it is not always fully achieved. We were fortunate to have a large site and an architectural team who believed in and, in fact, needed a symmetrical building because of its city axis. Thus the massing and the early layouts reflected a cruciform stage format but, at that time, without the six-stage spaces that ultimately became the format. Scenery handling and the loading bay took up only one part of the stage area and the rehearsal spaces were located at higher levels and consequently had significant problems with scenery transportation. At one time the stage and auditorium were to be completely above grade and the scenery, equipment, costumes, instruments, and people, were all to be raised and lowered. There were to be two large truck elevators with all the problems of restricted access and potential delays, remembering that this house would not have in-house workshops, other than those required for maintenance. Finally, an understanding of the extent of the servicing required to operate a building of this type led to the consultants successfully championing the stage and scene dock being set at tailboard height. This is almost the perfect situation because scenery and equipment deliveries can be effectively direct onto stage.

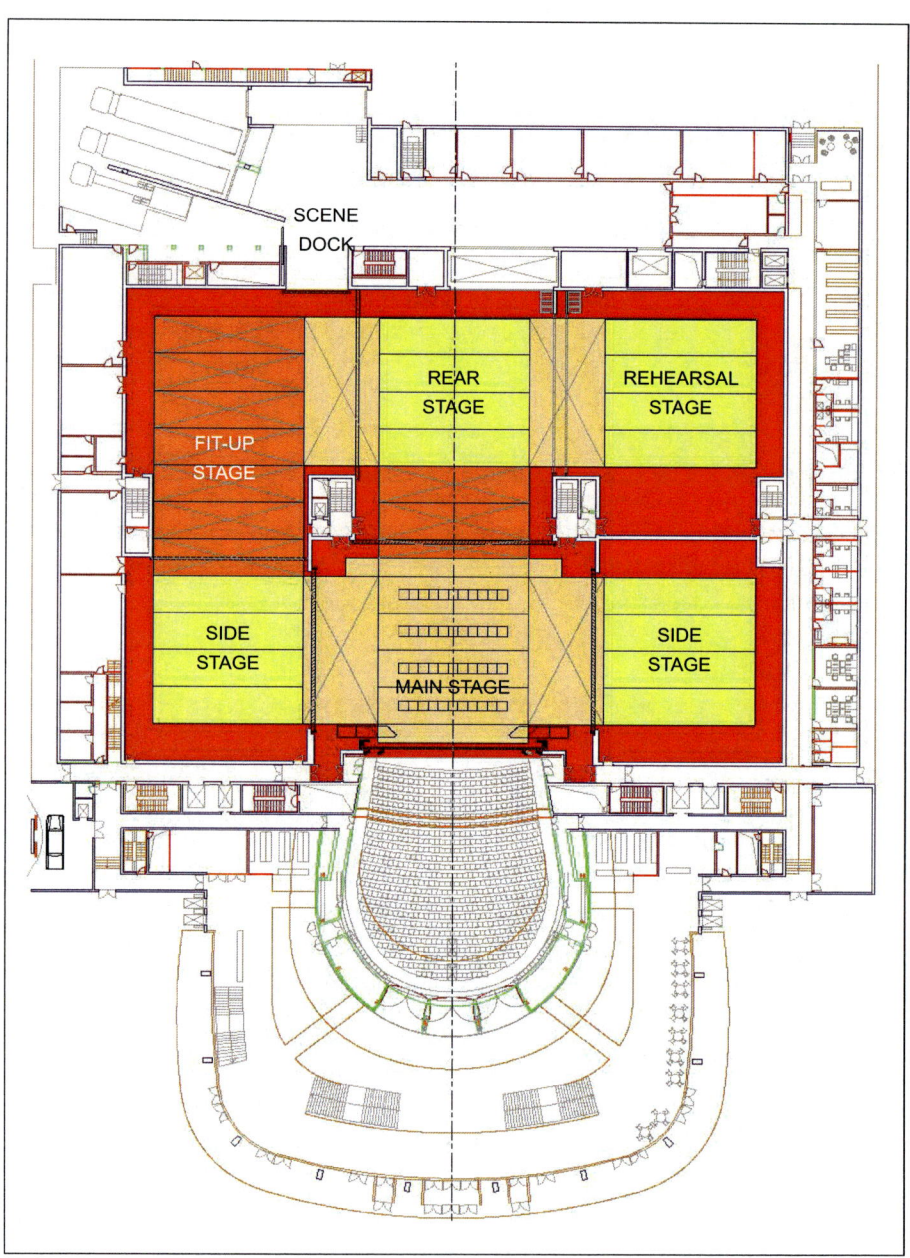

Plan on stage level.

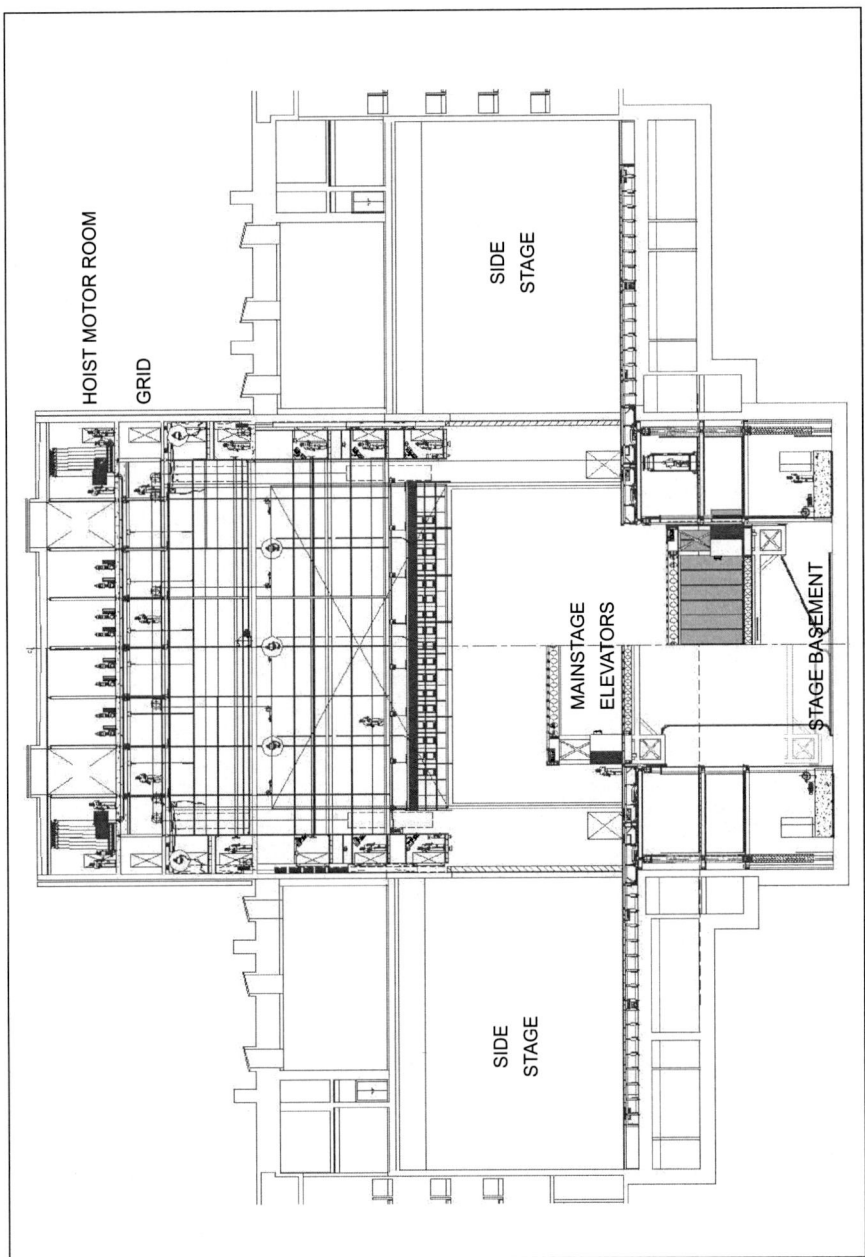

Cross section through stage and side stages.

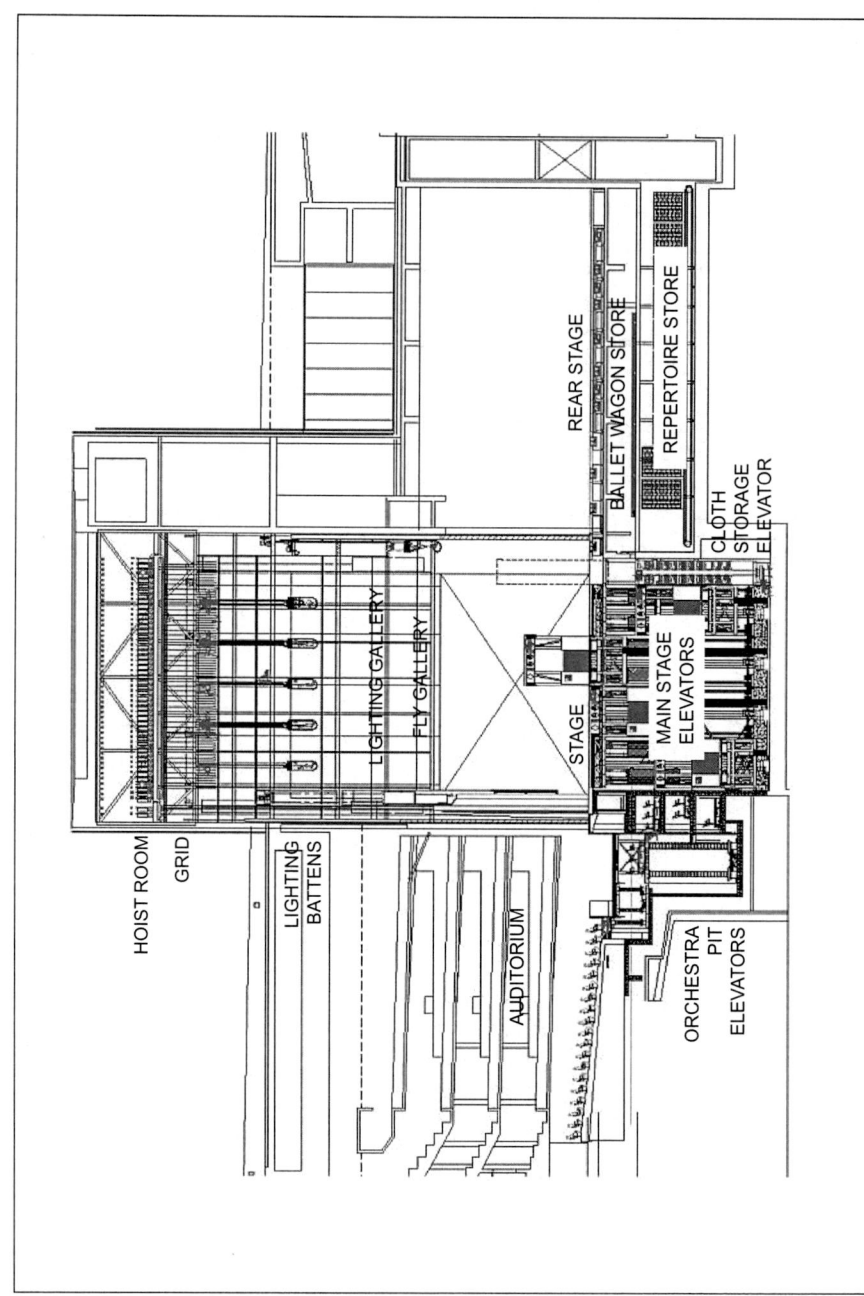

A long section through stage and fly tower.

Once the need for easy access of full-height scenery to a rehearsal stage was appreciated by the architects, the layout with five supporting spaces around the main stage, for which we had been pressing, became accepted. The two rear-side stages became a fit-up stage and a rehearsal stage. This allows excellent scenery movements (the need for a full stage wagon system had been established early in the planning) and enables a new setting to be erected and moved into the rehearsal stage early on in the production process. When required this setting can be brought out and used on the main stage, being returned to the rehearsal stage or placed in a side stage when required for more rehearsals or for performances in the repertoire.

An early decision was to set a 'clear scenery height' and maintain it absolutely throughout the scenery areas. The designers of a number of recent opera houses have not appreciated the necessity of the appropriate scenic height on stage and have failed to provide either side stages or other scenery spaces of adequate height. The designers, workshops and crew in the Finnish National Opera achieve amazing settings but have to hinge the tops of many of their scenic pieces in order to get them off-stage. Fitting flown tops to tall scenery is a nightmare and a further operational cost which should be avoided. After taking our planning experiences at Covent Garden and in Barcelona into account, it was decided to fix 11m as the scenery height in Copenhagen. Thus 11.2 metres became the 'clear height' and all structure, services and other overhead equipment was set above this level. Fortunately a floor level at 15.4 metres above stage had been detailed by the architects and this created a suitable overhead void for such facilities.

On the basis that all scenery coming out of trucks and containers was essentially 'horizontal', the loading bay and adjacent scene dock were made only 4.5 metres high. Served by two full size truck bays (one with a dock leveller) and a third smaller bay, this area receives all the scenery, properties, costumes, instruments, equipment and other supplies needed by the opera and ballet and touring theatre companies. Limited local storage of timber and metal sections is provided for the maintenance workshops. One truck bay is fitted with a long overhead rail with four 1 tonne chain hoists primarily for the off-loading of long scenery cloths, but which is also helpful for handling other items from open top vehicles. This was particularly useful during the delivery of the rolling cyclorama!

These facilities are extended for erecting scenery in the fit-up stage, rear stage and one side stage where there are five large overhead rolling beams, each carrying three 1-tonne chain hoists. Experience has shown that fewer larger hoists are generally more effective in these situations than a multiplicity of small units or flown bars. Three of the beams can move under power from the fit-up stage into the side stage and the other two remain in the rear stage. There is a rolling smoke curtain between the fit-up stage and the rear stage and one between the fit-up stage and the side stage. There are primarily for emergency use but can be lowered if required, for example, to mask lights from another area during a scene change. There is an interlock between the overhead cranes which move between the side stage and fit-up stage and that rolling smoke curtain so that collisions can be avoided, but it is not really practicable to achieve automatic collision prevention between the lowering fire curtain and any scenery below. There are times when only the skill and experience of the technical crew will provide the solution!

Vehicle being unloaded.

Chain hoists in loading bay.

Side stage crane hoists.

Dividing the Spaces
This excellent layout of side and rear stage spaces did lead to a re-evaluation of the sound and light separation necessary between them. At one stage the architect's drawings were showing slots in the floor above all of the side and rear stages, which were to accommodate vertically-moving shutters to divide up side, side-rear, rear and rehearsal stages. These slots were giving the architects major planning problems as the doors had to raise 11.2 metres and were having to pass through most of the accommodation around the fly tower. These doors were to be in addition to the three large dividing shutters around the main stage which rise up within the fly tower.

While it would occasionally be helpful to have sound-reducing doors between all the side and rear stages, it is a fact that the only area which it is essential to isolate, in addition to the main stage, is the rehearsal stage. It became quite impossible to plan the higher levels of the building effectively with these additional shutters passing through them. Also, large single-panel sound shutters are quite expensive and the elimination of two of these did help the budget. We were also determined to maintain a coherent flooring throughout all the stage scenery areas and rejected the idea of doors rising out of the floor or hoisting up to be folded flat on the ceiling.

One of the ideas we felt would be appropriate to isolating the rehearsal stage was to use proprietary interlocking panel doors on tracks, which are produced by a number of manufacturers. While such doors are manually operated and take a short while to open or close, the need to move scenery into or out of the rehearsal stage is not a frequent occurrence. Enquiries for a previous project had indicated that this type of door was only really workable up to 9, or maybe 10, metres but, when we pushed hard enough, we found that there were doors available to provide 50 dB separation in panels up to 11.2 metres high! Two sets of these doors separated by 1.5 metres provide 63 dB separation and are able to be opened and stacked away in about 10 minutes to let a full stage wagon through. A far shorter time is required when only a few panels have to be moved from each section to get a small piece of scenery or furniture in or out. When the large doors are closed there is access through personnel doors and a sound lobby to the rear stage.

Rehearsal stage door panels.

The left-hand side stage as you look at the audience (British stage left or prompt, or 'Queen' side in Denmark) is an enclosed space and is the side stage most used for storage of complete sets required in the rep. Like all 'dead' side stages this one cannot be easily serviced other than through the main stage, but plays an essential role as a store for a fully-erected opera set. The other side stage (OP or 'King') connects directly to both the fit-up stage and the rear stage. Money had been allowed for some roller curtains between each of these spaces, largely so that the side and rear stage could be darkened, and later in the project, as the fire strategy developed, these became the two rolling smoke curtains.

Rehearsal stage door.

Detail of stacking track for rehearsal stage door panels.

When these were originally installed the Scandinavian contractor was very nervous about operating them and we then discovered that he had miss-interpreted the Employer's Requirements. The smoke curtains he had installed could only be operated once and then required the attendance of an engineer to wind them up again and to reset them! Not quite what we or the theatre had wanted or described in the documents! The curtains were modified and are now able to be raised and lowered but are restricted to operation by authorised personnel. The curtains provide a light break between the areas but management must ensure that any noisy work stops in these areas during rehearsals or performances on stage before either of the two large sound-reducing dividing doors are opened.

Smoke curtain between fit-up and rear stages.

The three large dividing doors (shutters) and the safety curtain were manufactured by Delstar Engineering from the UK. These doors each weigh about 28 tonnes and are counterweighted. They are hauled up by a pair of double-purchased wire ropes winding onto two drums, one each side of a central gearbox. The contractors were given the option of achieving the required 45dB sound reduction by using sealing motion, acoustic labyrinths or pneumatic seals. Following the same practice as in the Royal Opera House, Delstar opted for pneumatic seals but found that these were not as easy to employ as may be thought. The doors operate well but take rather longer to unseal than expected and all available expertise has failed to speed up this operation. Covent Garden experience indicated that it is not always necessary to seal the doors when they are closed and so the sealing and unsealing operations were separated from door motion and the push button station now indicates when the seals have retracted.

In order to allow the orchestra to rehearse in the pit while work proceeds on stage, the safety curtain also has a sound reduction index of 45dB. The structural proscenium opening in the theatre is 20 metres wide and has a height of 12 metres which made this curtain quite a giant. It is counterweighted at both ends and raised and lowered by a similar double-drum hoist unit mounted on the downstage part of the grid structure. When testing its emergency release, the noise of the mechanism and hydraulic controller was like a screaming banshee but that didn't prevent the fire authorities requiring an additional 105dB siren to warn of its descent!

Dividing door hoist unit showing the double winding drums.

In fact all four of these heavy vertically-moving doors and the smoke curtains can be released remotely from a security panel in the stage door area. This was a feature the theatre consultants were not enthusiastic about, preferring that the fire-brigade established the situation on the ground before lowering these doors. The safety curtain is likely to be clear of scenery but that situation may not apply to the other doors or smoke curtains. Although the fire authorities visited Covent Garden and other theatres to see how other regulators handle matters, there are, as so often happens, a number of local variations on theatre fire strategy in different countries.

Moving the Scenery Around

The theatre consultant team had significant experience of stage wagon systems having studied many but having also planned both the Gran Teatre del Liceu in Barcelona and that in the Royal Opera House in London. Much time was spent with Jeff Phillips in Covent Garden considering all aspects of the side-driven wagons conceived by Mike Barnett for that installation. This is described in some detail by Clive Odom in Volume 2 of *Theatre Engineering and Architecture: Engineering and Technology* published by the ABTT.

The principle on which a real stage wagon system has to be based is that it should provide a completely level floor at all times. Therefore, the floor has to consist of elevators of the same plan size as the wagons. An elevator is lowered to allow a wagon to move on to it and the elevator vacated by a wagon is then raised. The stage wagons move over lowered elevators. These elevators are referred to as equalisers or compensators – in the Copenhagen project the wagon-sized elevators are called equalisers while the larger sections of floor each side of the main stage and each side of the rear stage are referred to as compensators. An additional half-wagon without an equaliser beneath it in the most downstage position enables the settings on wagons to extend downstage through the portal to the house curtain line.

Basically the Royal Opera House stage wagon system employs passive wagons moved by mechanisms fitted into the equalisers or fixed flooring adjacent to the wagon. This means that there are no guide- or drive-tracks and the only gaps are those between wagons. The wagons are guided by their edges, travelling as they do in a 'canal' between lowered equalisers or alongside a section of fixed floor. One of the disadvantages of this installation is that, because the drives for the stage wagons are in the sides of the equaliser elevators, these elevators have to be raised adjacent to any wagon or group of wagons which is to move. This is not a problem except that the equalisers have to lift the weight of a stage wagon and possibly the full load of scenery on that wagon. As part of the analysis of wagon drive systems the economics of this in an installation of 26 equalisers had to be considered. Also, while the hydraulics used in the Royal Opera House to raise and lower the equalisers and to disengage the drive cassettes work fine, our client in Copenhagen was not keen on us using hydraulics.

In order to service all the stage spaces the stage wagons have to move both up and down stage and across stage. In fact, in order to work fully for all theatrical settings, they move downstage of their normal across-stage line when onstage so that the setting can continue down almost to the line of the house curtain. They have to carry significant loads statically and dynamically and be able to be positioned accurately. Like the equaliser platforms they also have to be very accurately dimensioned so that any wagon will fit into any position. The wagons are therefore jig-built steel frames mounted on special castor wheels with a large part of their central flooring removable for traps. These special castors (turtles or 'triple-

Triple swivel castor unit.

swivel castors' as they are known in the theatre industry) consist of three swivel castors mounted on a rotating steel plate. As the wagon is pulled at 90° or in the opposite direction to that in which it was travelling, the triple swivel castors rotate within the wagon and minimise the lateral motion that one experiences with normal trolley castors. The real secret of the Copenhagen and Barcelona triple-swivel castors is that each of the three castors is a double-wheeled unit. These often counter-rotate when the forces require it, reducing scuffing and further easing the change of direction.

After much analysis we determined that a fully loaded stage wagon of the type we wanted could be moved over its own length by only two or three drives. We also considered where these might be most effectively placed and how they might best operate. An important principle to remember with a stage wagon system is that the wagons, generally, form the stage floor and are the surface on which the performance, be it opera, ballet or drama, takes place. Therefore, we felt it may be practicable to fit stage wagon drives in the floor surface rather than at the sides because the drives on stage would normally be hidden underneath a wagon. We also wanted to continue the principle of the wagons being guided by travelling in a 'canal'.

We developed the new concept of a pinion drive which is mounted in the floor and which rises to engage in a pin rack mounted in the underside of the stage wagons. This rack had to be offset to

Pinion sketch indicating one of the many raising/lowering mechanisms investigated.

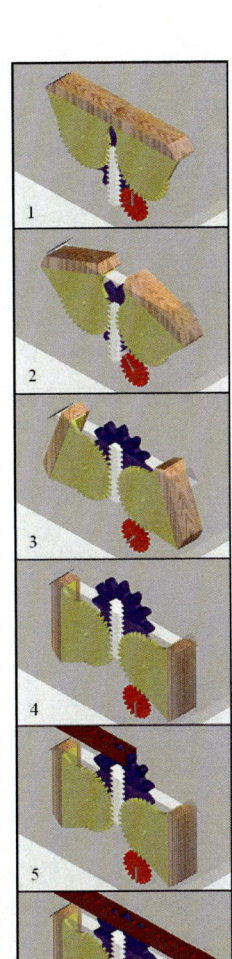

One of the early wagon drive CAD models showing a timber cover which opens and the blue pinion rising to mesh with the approaching rack attached to the stage wagon.

Copenhagen Opera House 121

allow for the removable traps in the centre of each wagon. The positions of the pinions were set out full size on the floor of the office and we determined that, compared with many other opera house stages, the obstruction and visibility of these drives would be minimal. The original pinion was slender and was raised and lowered through a narrow slot. This principle was developed further and set out in the Employer's Requirements along with drawings and detailed performance parameters.

A prototype of the Royal Opera House system had been built and tested before the installation was fabricated and a similar provision was made in the Copenhagen tender documents. In addition to the development of the rising pinion drive, one complete wagon, 16 x 4 metres, was to be constructed and demonstrated moving in two directions (along and at right angles to its length) under various loads up to its maximum. This contract was won by Waagner-Biro (UK) Ltd who, under their then new management, set about enthusiastically creating a suitable drive unit. This performed well under test on the bench and enabled a reduction in motor size to be agreed and a number of other refinements to be made. Some very good developments of the pinion, of the raise-lower mechanism and the addition of a metal cover which closes the slot when the pinion lowered resolved most of the outstanding concerns. Waagner-Biro also demonstrated the principles of the control system which needs to know where a given wagon is and to raise and synchronise the pinion with the moving rack as a wagon approaches a drive. The racks became fully-machined involute-cut gear racks rather than pin racks for greater accuracy and a quieter drive.

The full-size wagon test was a great success. Apart from one of the site

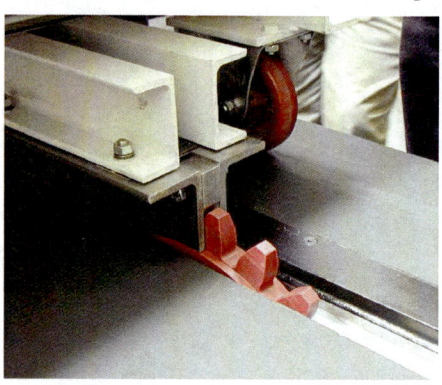

Tests on wagon drive principle.

Installed wagon drive unit from underneath.

project managers, quite reasonably, checking the effect of putting his foot on a rotating pinion and tripping the laser detector early, the wagon operated with only minor problems in both directions and, surprisingly, without any side restraints. The development of the pinion had introduced a shoulder below the shaped drive teeth and this provided sufficient guidance to hold the wagons in line. As the wagons were now being driven by at least two staggered drives, one at each end or one at each side of the wagon depending on direction of motion, the Waagner-Biro engineers had the ability to adjust their relative motion slightly and to re-align the motion of a wagon. This was a great freedom and overcame the potential problem of wagons moving across the compensators where they were not always going to have a full side restraint. In fact, under test on site later, wagons were often moved long distances without any adjacent restraints and still ended up accurately between two raised equalisers.

Pinions fabricated in steel and of cast nylon were both tested and it was agreed that the nylon should be used because of the high cost and difficulty of replacing a length of damaged machined rack, compared to the cost of a replacement pinion.

Drive pinion raised through floor.

Stage wagons moving across rear stage under test.

Stage wagons moving up-down stage without 'crabbing'.

Access to the pinions for maintenance is available by lifting the surrounding timber floor panel. Each of the pinion drive units is identical, although the specified process of aligning these was not fully implemented. All parties now agree that more accurate setting up of the drives and the local laser position sensors in the factory and more rigorous site alignment would have expedited the completion of the commissioning process. How often have we heard these views expressed in stage engineering, but always after the event! In fact, the degree of control now demonstrable is awesome and some of the lessons learned by the consultants and the commissioning engineers could not have been appreciated without a prototype of all six stages and a far longer programme! At least this expertise is available for the next comprehensive stage wagon installation.

Stage wagons moving with scenery.

One use for damaged pinions!

A characteristic of a number of Scandinavian theatres is the 'revolve'. The 'Old Stage' in the Royal Theatre itself is a revolving structure with a number of traps and small elevators fitted within it. The stage of the City Theatre in Helsinki is similar, although a more recent construction, and this rotates on a thin film of grease rather than on bearings or on peripheral wheels. We were under pressure to provide a revolving stage in line with this practice.

We wanted this revolve in the opera to be in a wagon so that could be used efficiently, rather than a unit that had to be fitted-up on the main stage elevators and then lowered to be level with the stage floor. The overall height of the wagons had been determined by the minimum necessary depth of structure and triple-swivel castors and had been set at 300 mm. Not wanting the revolve wagon to be any higher, we began examining ways in which a revolving stage could be constructed in this limited depth. It soon became clear that it was impracticable to design this conventionally with the revolve running on circular tracks supported within a square wagon frame. There was not enough depth to get any form of multi-directional castor under the supports of the circular tracks. Having already developed a wagon that could in theory rotate, because of the ability of the triple-swivel castors to accommodate any direction of travel, we proposed making the centre circle of the wagon a full-height revolving platform supported on triple-swivel castors. As there was no fixed structure in the centre, this circular section would be held in position by horizontally-mounted peripheral wheels. The revolve could be driven at its periphery either by a toothed belt or a friction drive and Waagner-Biro opted for friction, based on the success of their previous installations.

The revolving stage based on this principle works well. It moves around the stage within its square 16 x 16m wagon unit and, when

Revolving stage under full-load test.

Revolve wagon structure showing break line through revolve and frame.

Revolve drive motors.

Ballet wagon being moved from its store onto the four lowered elevators. *The ballet wagon frame awaiting its floor in its store under the rear stage.*

plugged up to its special drive and with the wagon locked in position, it revolves quite smoothly, although it is important to ensure that the surface of the stage is clean and free from any debris. The revolve has been rotated during a Puccini aria and even the acoustic consultant was happy afterwards! The wagon must be locked in position by the adjoining raised equalisers or compensators as the reaction forces from the rotation will try to rotate the whole wagon unit. The revolve is provided with a central trap and a number of other traps that align with those in the main stage elevators in both the normal and most downstage positions of the wagons. Just to add to the excitement, the revolve can be locked in position within the wagon unit and this un-bolted to form two separate 16 x 8 metre wagons for use when no revolve effects are required in the repertoire.

There is another special wagon, this one carrying the permanent dance floor. This is also 16 x 16 metres and is driven in exactly the same way as the other wagons. It has a special store under the rear stage from where it can be brought up to stage level on the main stage elevators. This is particularly effective as it allows the dance floor to be put into service and removed without affecting what is in either of the side stages or the rear stage. The ballet floor is constructed on a homogeneous plane of 15 mm plywood mounted on special neoprene pads at 300 mm centres. The resilience of the pads matches that of the plywood over the span and provides a suitable dance floor for ballet. The timber floor is normally covered with a Harlequin Studio dance floor surface in grey and is not intended for heavy sets or rough treatment. It is also important that the flooring is laid to a high standard with all the joints correctly aligned and glued. In the Royal Opera House the dance floor wagons are painted red and clearly labelled to try to prevent damage to the floors. That has not been done in Copenhagen but it is hoped that its special store, which is only high enough to clear its depth, will prevent it being used incorrectly.

The Space Understage

The equipment described so far has provided for efficient and practical erection and movement of scenery around the stage, and into both the scenic rehearsal room and onto the stage. When on stage, rather more can happen to it!

The range of main stage elevators that you find in opera houses is considerable. From the multiple-elevator modular approach in the Carlo Felice Theatre in Genoa and in the Budapest National Theatre, through the compromise techniques necessary in Barcelona, to the major hydraulic double-deck elevators in the Metropolitan Opera House, they all have to serve the designer, performer and director. Thus we set about deciding what would provide the appropriate level of facility. Clearly the elevators had to raise and lower the stage wagons, both with and without scenery, but how far? To what

Stage elevators raised.

Lower platform lowered.   *Lower platform raised.*

extent should we eliminate structure to permit greater theatrical use? Should the elevators have raking tops? Are double level elevators really useful? And how should they be operated to achieve the minimum noise?

These and other questions took a great deal of thought. We had previously planned elevators with a large clear span for the lyric theatre in the extension to the Megaron in Athens and this principle had considerable appeal, although a double-deck elevator does really require to be quite deep if the lower platform is going to be useful scenically. Then it becomes difficult to use it effectively for access through traps and other effects. Raking mechanisms complicate elevators and there are difficulties to be overcome such as eliminating gaps when adjacent elevator tops are raked. From a careful consideration of the anticipated auditorium sightlines, and the ways in which the elevators could be engineered and might be used, we established that the elevators ought to have a travel of at least 10 metres, from 5 metres below to 5 metres above stage level.

Designs were prepared for four identical elevators, all with this full travel as we could see no economic benefit in limiting the travel of one or more. The top platforms are fixed to end structures which carry the guides and wire-rope pick-up points and these platforms do not rake but remain horizontal. After all, with a stage wagon system, the principle must be to build any rake required on the stage wagon so that it can be properly dressed while off stage and can also used in the rehearsal stage. The opening between the side structures of the elevators is 11.6 metres giving a useful width of under-floor scene which can be raised into view. This implied that the internal floor within the elevator would have to be around 5 metres below the top platform making the use of actors' elevators and other equipment rather difficult. The solution to this problem was to hang the lower platform, and the access doors at each end,

Stage elevator raised showing the height available for an internal setting.

on suspended screw-jacks so that it could be raised when necessary within the elevator frame, up to about 2.5 metres below stage. The stage engineering contractor, Waagner-Biro from Austria on this contract, manufactured, installed and commissioned this equipment to a very high standard. But early on, one of the company's representatives, not fully understanding the use of stage equipment, was quite content to try and omit this important feature of the moving lower platform on cost grounds!

The four elevators can each carry 48 tonnes statically and 32 tonnes in motion. They are partially counterweighted and travel at a maximum speed of 250 mm/sec. They have their own engineering control system, but can also be operated by the stage control system using the same desks as control the overstage flying.

Cloth Storage

Even with the advent of acrylic paints and cloths that can be folded for storage there is still a requirement for the quick storage of rolled cloths and other long items. The technique followed here was to include a cloth store elevator upstage of the main stage elevators. An equaliser elevator was already needed

Removing the bin trolley from the cloth storage elevator.

Cloth storage elevator raised.

here as part of the overall stage wagon circulation so this unit was split into two, each 2 metres wide, the most downstage being the cloth store. Sixteen metres width was insufficient for cloths (the bars are all 22 metres long) so the cloth storage elevator is 23 metres wide.

Unusually, the cloth storage elevator has another function. It has to travel below the stage to the level where the ballet wagon is stored under the rear stage as otherwise the ballet wagon would have to pass through it to get on to the main stage elevators which pass this level in their normal travel. So that no greater width of opening than that of the main stage elevators was created, the side sections of floor on the cloth storage elevator, outside the central 16 metres, remain at stage level when it lowers, but are carried up on the elevator when this is raised above stage.

The cloth storage elevator has shelves which take cloth bins which are, in fact, just frames to contain rolled and long materials. This followed from the cloth storage system in the existing Royal Theatre in Copenhagen. Stored just beneath the floor of the elevator are two long trolleys either of which can be taken out, depending on which side of the store one wishes to use, and these can be aligned with the storage bins which stop at pre-set levels. The elevator travels at 9 metres/minute normally but reducing the pressure on the press-and-hold button will cause it to slow down to half speed and stop with the next bin level with the top of the trolley. The bin may then be transferred to the trolley and taken to the position of the flying sets.

Cloth storage bin on trolley.

Spiralifts for cloth store.

The cloth storage elevator rises about 7½ metres – higher than the main stage elevators – and contains eight shelves either side giving a significant storage capacity of up to 20 tonnes. In view of this payload and the weight of the structure necessary to carry it, the lifting mechanism is a set of six 18" Spiralifts.

The Proscenium Zone

To accommodate a wide range of proscenium openings, the Opera has both what was dubbed an 'architectural proscenium' and a portal or 'false proscenium'. The architectural proscenium is effectively in the auditorium (it is on the stage front) and intended as the continuation of the room around the proscenium. Within this opening and set upstage of the house curtain is the portal which sets the opening to the scene. Both the architectural proscenium and the portal are adjustable in height and width, enabling the architectural opening to be reduced partially when a small portal is in use, thus reducing the amount of black portal which is visible. The width of the architectural proscenium is manually adjusted to set positions, although the header is motorised. The side portions carry side lighting and a number of loudspeakers.

Downstage view showing portal and architectural proscenium.

The architectural proscenium is a larger version of the 'barley sugars' in the Royal Opera House, Covent Garden: the Copenhagen proscenium can be moved on and off stage by some 2 metres each side.

The portal consists of a full-width double-deck lighting bridge and two suspended towers. The towers hang either side of the bridge, which links to both side galleries. The bridge is raised and lowered by a hoist unit driving a number of double-purchase suspensions. The hoist is mounted on fixed structure above the top position of the bridge. Portals take up valuable downstage space and do tend to push the setting line upstage, but they have an important lighting and masking function. Here we made the portal bridge as narrow as practicable in order to minimise the lost space and the balance appears good. Equipment mounted too far outside the lighting bridge bounce bars will be hit either by a flown cloth or that outside the towers may be struck by scenery on a moving wagon if this is erected on the downstage edge but these are production design matters that cannot be eliminated by the consultant. Better to have good contact between performer, orchestra and audience and compromise this when needed for a particular lighting requirement or

A heavily rigged tormentor tower.

setting than to be restricted for ever. Good acoustics are also ensured by covering the whole of the portal in Gerriets *Echovelour,* a velour material which absorbs light but which has a higher reflectivity in the audible frequency range than normal scenic velours. The facing on the returns of the portal are particularly important acoustic reflection surfaces.

The proscenium zone has other secrets. One of these is the unusual placing of the rolling cyclorama storage. Rolling cycloramas have always been a problem in that, whether placed upstage or downstage, they take up valuable stage space. Looking at this problem anew, we decided that the only free space of full height in the fly tower was downstage of the portal, either side of the house curtain. By planning the stage area carefully we had gained sufficient overall width to accommodate the full portal tower movement offstage and this extra width offered a position for the rolling cyclorama.

However, hanging the cyclorama roll in this position would block access past the house curtain. We then determined that we should raise the cyclorama cone a short distance to allow passage under the cyclorama when stored. But there is another feature of even the best

Portal bridge hoist installation.

Downstage obstruction caused by rolling cyclorama in the Royal Theatre.

Rolling cyclorama being delivered to the new Opera.

rolling cycloramas and that is that they take time to deploy and to wind away into storage. Developing our concept to overcome this problem led to both the storage cone and cyclorama track being able to be raised and lowered about 5.2 metres by four dedicated winches. This not only allows passage onstage in the downstage zone but also enables the deployed cyclorama to be raised to allow cast, technicians and properties to be moved on and off stage rapidly. As the cyclorama is also wound on and off the cone when raised, the bottom edge of the cloth does not scrape on the stage floor, and it being 5.2 metres overhead allows much preparatory work to go on before it is finally lowered. Not having to clear the whole stage was

Cyclorama roll being raised into position.

Copenhagen Opera House 135

Rolling cyclorama extended and hanging above elevators awaiting flooring.

certainly useful during commissioning! And for those who believe that the cyclorama should go right up to the underside of the grid we must point out that, in practical terms, the view of the audience even in the front stalls is not compromised.

The cyclorama cloth was manufactured and painted by Gerriets in France and shipped along the canals and by sea to Copenhagen. The timber container was 25 metres long but, because of the space in the scene dock and the direct access to the stage, the unloading and installing of the cyclorama was very straightforward. The hauling rope was damaged during some of the early commissioning moves but, while a replacement took some time to obtain and replace, no further difficulties were encountered. The cone is fabricated in aluminium and moves up and down a central screw as it rotates to maintain the alignment of the rope in the groove. The hauling rope is tensioned by weights and hauled by a special winch mounted above the portal in the grid.

In order that the cyclorama cloth can pass from its storage position to where it needs to hang upstage beneath the track, there is a gap between the portal

Cyclorama on cone mounted downstage of portal.

Upstage suspended frame for cyclorama track.

and the galleries through which it passes. Access to the portal on the actors' left side is therefore not possible while the cyclorama is being moved, but at all other times it is possible to step across the gap. The cyclorama cloth is protected when passing through the gap by strips of UMHWPE plastic. The only modification which we would make on future installations would be to level the track before winding the cyclorama in or out. The track slopes down by 2½° upstage in order to make the corners hang correctly and this does cause some bunching of the cloth as it moves onto the cone. With the hoisting system incorporated into the present design this slope could be eliminated by differential raising of the upstage and downstage hoists.

Because of the nature of the repertoire and the range of shows which will be staged in the Opera, we included a house curtain which can fly out, draw horizontally and swag in the Italian style. This uses Triple-E chain track with proportional-fold bobbins for its drawing mechanism, a fast flying hoist and a separate hoist mounted in the motor room above the grid for the swagging motion. The swagging rope which passes through the curtain rings is Kevlar

View of house curtain swagged.

and this connects to a steel wire rope for winding onto the drum. One of the problems which had to be solved was ensuring sufficient travel for the joining shackle without meeting a pulley. When flying out the house curtain the control system knows to wind the swagging hoist at the same speed so that the swagging lines do not droop. The house curtain has its own local controls although it can also be operated as part of a power flying or stage elevator cue using the stage control system.

The Orchestra Pit

The orchestra pit is a very important area in any opera house and it took a lot of architect, acoustician, mechanical services engineer and theatre consultant time to resolve the many conflicts. The orchestra pit in Copenhagen needed to be able to accommodate up to one hundred and four musicians for large-scale opera such as *Electra* but also had to be able to be made smaller for many other operas and for ballet. The brief also calls for there to be no pit at all should any production in the house not require an orchestra. To achieve

Orchestra pit being set up.

Seating wagons being moved during installation.

this, the orchestra pit has three separate elevators and thirteen movable seating wagons that can be positioned to extend the stalls seating towards the stage when either a smaller pit, or no pit, is required.

The seating wagons which carry the extra stalls seating need to be stored when not in use, and this is usually achieved by creating a storage area beneath the stalls floor. In Copenhagen we were unable to accommodate such a storage area, as the area below the stalls was already designated for the orchestra rehearsal room. This only left a narrow strip of space between the orchestra pit and the main stage elevators. We therefore created three levels of seating wagon storage, one below the other, in this area. Further storage was provided by a lower platform in one of the three elevators.

In order to access these storage areas, the orchestra pit elevator nearest to the stage had to be built with two platforms. The top platform of this elevator can rise up to stage level so that it can be used as a forestage. In this condition, hidden doors in each of the side walls can be opened and used for access to the forestage. This elevator may be moved downwards until the top level reaches the top storage level. The lower platform on this elevator can be positioned at either of the two lower storage levels. The overall travel of this elevator is 7220 mm. There are two further elevators, both of which are a single platform. The one adjacent to the double deck elevator carries two rows of seats and has limited travel of 1250 mm. The second, furthest from the stage is for a single row of seats and has a similar travel. After the seating wagons on the near stage elevator are moved into store, the elevators can be aligned and other wagons can be moved onto the near stage elevator for movement into store. In fact, the seating on the near stage elevator is only infrequently used and this is shunted into an intermediate level and then moved on the lower deck of the elevator into the lowest store. This simplifies the more frequent changes between normal and large orchestra pit formats.

The orchestra pit rail consists of twenty short sections which fit to the

Seating wagons on near-stage elevator and in store (on right).

Near-stage seating wagon in store.

Seating wagons stored on lower platform of near-stage elevator.

An orchestra pit balustrade section on movement trolley.

front of the fixed stalls seating or to the seating wagons so as to form the curved balustrade. The rail is divided into sections to enable it to be handled and moved into position. The frames for the rail sections were made by Waagner-Biro (UK), who also installed the orchestra pit elevators, and then these were finished by the auditorium interior fitters to details developed by the acousticians and architects. The installation includes a pair of trolleys which are used to lift the balustrade sections off and move them to a new location. The finished balustrade sections are heavy and not as easy to move around on their low-friction bases as had been planned so the trolleys are used more intensively in some changeovers. If all the seats are used the balustrade sections are stored in one of the seating stores.

There are thirteen separate seating wagons. These include three wagons making up a single row which is removed to form the very large pit. With these in place the normal opera pit is created. Four more wagons each carry three rows of seats and when in place reduce the pit to a size more suitable for an orchestra for ballet. The remaining six wagons together create another three rows of seats and when in place eliminate any pit or forestage.

All the wagons are fitted with air castors which work in a similar way to a Hovercraft but use an air bearing developed to pass over small gaps or changes in level in the floor. These have individual air blowers which blow air through small holes in a rubber membrane to lift the wagon some 15-20 mm above the floor. This allows the heavy wagons to be pushed into position by two or three people, either when moving them on the elevators or in the storage areas. The seating wagons are finished with the same hardwood flooring and seats as the rest of the auditorium, and once in position, blend in so well that it is not apparent that they are not a permanent part of the stalls area.

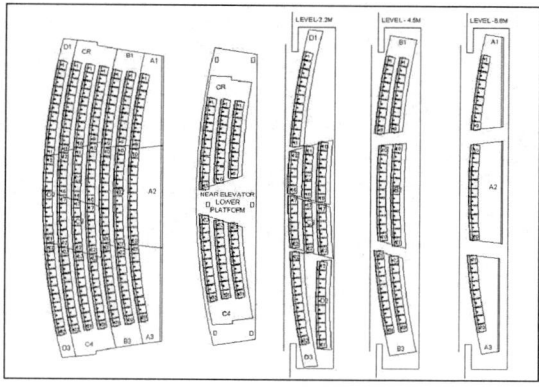

Diagram of seating wagon layout and storage zones.

One of the difficulties in every orchestra pit is providing suitable, draught-free, ventilation at the right temperature for the musicians. There are many solutions in use world-wide, each of which has its proponents, and after considerable debate the use of a number of large air grilles in the floor was proposed by the engineers. The floor of the pit already had a number of lighting,

Construction of seating wagons showing the air bearings.

power and audio outlet traps in it. It also had to be able to feature as a forestage and to provide a coherent surface over which the air bearings could move the very heavy seating wagons. Once again the theatre consultant was faced with finding a solution. We developed a triangular 'Toblerone' unit with a grille which dropped slightly, rotated some 120° and raised a solid timber flooring section in place of the grille. The third face was open to allow air clear passage to the grille. Waagner-Biro developed the principle into a two-sided unit with air passage each side which rotated 180° and achieved the same result with a clever gear rack and pinion. These were installed in the floor and enable the grilles to be removed automatically before the seating wagons are moved across or the elevators are raised to create a forestage. It is particularly important that the elevator floor is without grilles when used as a forestage. For this function it also has three large manually-removable traps in its centre as well as numerous hinged openings hiding lighting and sound outlets.

The double deck elevator is raised and lowered by means of Serapid rigid chains which form vertical columns beneath the elevator. The basic principle is simple – the chain is stored horizontally in covered channels mounted on the

The rotating grille mechanism.

Rotating grille in place.

Rotating grille in motion.

Rotating grille with floor panel in place.

The eight Serapid chains which raise and lower the near-stage elevator.

floor of the elevator pit, pinions are rotated by a motor which drives the chains through 90 degrees in a special housing forcing the links to lock and form a rigid pushing bar, thus applying thrust to the elevator structure.

Mid and far elevator screw-jack drives showing the special scissor guides.

The elevator is guided over its travel distance so that the chains are kept vertical and therefore cannot bend. The two single deck elevators are also electrically driven, although the mechanisms used for these are the more common screw jacks. These are more economic for this reduced travel and are able to be synchronised with the rigid chain elevator so that the level of the orchestra pit can be adjusted as a whole.

The Fly Tower

In determining the stage area planning, one of the early decisions was to prepare drawings to establish the likely worst-case sightlines and ensure that the stage could be masked using conventional legs and borders and still leave both an adequate playing space for the maximum portal opening and a suitable off-stage wing back to the side dividing door. After various design iterations we settled on an inside fly tower width of 30 metres which gave us an interesting geometric size for the off-stage compensator of 8 metres; double the wagon 'module' of 4 metres. Maintaining this geometric relationship was important to the success of the wagon installation and although we did have to loose the odd metre off the overall dimensions of each side stage, we did retain sufficient peripheral space here for the wagon drive cabinets and for striking and stacking scenery from the wagons. Some of this space has been used as quick-change rooms and for more permanent storage.

The fly tower height was based on 30 metres to the underside of the grid. While not always applicable (or properly understood!) this is in line with the rule of thumb that the fly tower should be 2½ times the proscenium height. In fact the structural opening is 12 metres, but it is a difficult rule to apply as the working portal height will vary from that in extremis, down to a more usual 8-10 metres. The 30 metre height was based on experience but does allow for the raise-lower rolling cyclorama and for flying out normal height cloths clear of overstage lighting.

The complement of galleries is, from lowest to highest, fly gallery, lighting gallery, rigging gallery, maintenance gallery and windlass gallery. Sockets for control of the flying system are provided on the lower two and upper two galleries, with lighting outlets on them all in suitable numbers. The lower galleries are all in steel and hung in a conventional way with an opening offstage for the dividing doors and their counterweights. We asked for the maintenance gallery to be concrete so that we could mount the dividing

Side stage left with quick-change rooms.

door hoists, head pulleys and other equipment on it, a decision that was vindicated later. In fact, next time we may have concrete enclosures built on this gallery for the dividing door hoists as they did prove difficult to silence to the acoustician's satisfaction!

The lighting gallery has DIN back-to-back channels with Danish standard luminaire mounting sockets mounted within them at half-metre centres. Although not initially requested we included 48 mm lighting pipes both under the DIN rails and at high level along all the galleries. The lower pipe is fitted with steel mesh safety panels when there are no luminaires in position and, despite being warned that 'our technicians don't kneel down' it's encouraging to see how much this useful low side lighting position is being used! Maybe it's due to the short-tuft industrial carpet which we find so appropriate and use on all our major theatre galleries!

The lowest galleries are installed each side of the fly tower at a height to clear scenery on the stage wagons or which is being otherwise moved on or off stage. There is no crossover upstage at this level as this space accommodates a dedicated back lighting frame on a hoist which flies it out to this level to allow scenery to pass under it from the rear stage. The lighting is also often used at this height. In order to pass from side to side at the lowest gallery level we introduced a gallery within the downstage part of the rear stage which allows for lighting if the rear stage is used as part of a setting and also provides a wonderful route for visitors where they can see activities backstage without getting in the way! The rigging gallery is a reduced version of the lighting gallery and this does have a cross-over upstage within the fly tower.

Lighting gallery from on stage.

Above the maintenance gallery is the windlass galley where the power and control feeds to the overstage lighting originate. This gallery is more of a machine room with remotely-starting machinery and so is not on the normal visitors' tour. It has proved to be an excellent solution to accommodating these electrical supplies. The drop cables, their connectors and the diverter pulleys can be withdrawn inside the gallery hangers when the windlasses are moved along the gallery to another position. The design allows for two windlasses to feed each full lighting frame. This provides two supplies of nearly 200A over three phases. If required a windlass can be directed to a special lighting suspension or more conventional 'tripe' can be rigged and used manually from the rigging gallery.

An area on which we lavished a lot of thought and attention was the grid and the installations therein. Having now seen a variety of theatre grids in numerous countries it is apparent that there are many grid installations that are not satisfactory and do not provide a clear working area. One of our schemes for a previous major theatre that had never been constructed was the concept that we followed and developed. This scheme had succeeded in eliminating much of the rigging and wiring associated with point hoists, leaving the grid uncluttered for access, manual rigging, lighting feeds and similar. Another

The windlass gallery.

General view of grid.

change was away from traditional British steel channel grids (which are fine if you need to clamp diverter pulleys to them and mount large point hoist frames on them) to a bi-directional grille with openings suitable to take a chain hoist load hook or a point hoist bob-weight. This is a lighter construction and, despite having a larger open area than the conventional steel channel grid, appears far less unsettling to those of a nervous disposition! It also enabled us to eliminate sprinkler pipes and heads from under the grid or, as seen in one recent installation, actually fitted on the grid floor.

Overstage Flying Systems

The flying system is based on flown across-stage bars, with some up-down stage bars each side and a number of point hoists. These are all controlled by the stage control system which is distributed and, in addition, controls the main stage elevators, the house curtain and the revolving stage in the stage wagon. The house curtain has its own control as well in each downstage corner. The wagons are subject to their own control system which is also interlocked with the stage control for safety and accidental damage prevention.

The Copenhagen Opera repeats the layout of the power flying installation in the Gran Teatre del Liceu, in that the hoists and their drive equipment are mounted in a room above grid level. A number of installations place the hoists at the side of the grid which either obstructs the galleries or widens the tower significantly and this is not always possible. In new construction, like the new fly tower in Barcelona and the complete building in Copenhagen, a motor room above the grid can fit into the planning well. When we first saw the Copenhagen plans with the enormous motor room above the grid but showing only the power flying hoists each side we did have some moments of concern! But this area then also became a major duct route for air to the auditorium and also served to accommodate the point hoists and one of the three fixed dimmer rooms.

Motor room before equipment installation started.

The rigging associated with the point hoists is restricted to overhead. The wire ropes pass vertically down from the hoists in the motor room above the grid, where they are located in the upstage and downstage zones, and over swivel diverter pulleys so as to travel up and down stage horizontally. They then pass over moveable diverter pulleys mounted on rolling beams which travel in each grid bay, between the wire rope drops to the multi-line flying sets. The moveable pulleys and rolling beams can be locked in positions which are numbered and which put the point hoist wire rope drop in the centre of each grille opening. The bob weight can be raised through the grid using local controls and hung under the pulley while this and the beam are moved to a new location thus minimising the effort required to re-rig a point suspension. A special rigger's control allows the encoder to be disengaged while a point is being moved and re-engaged when the bob-weight is again hanging at a marked height just below the grid. This ensures that the overall travel is not exceeded in either direction. The rolling beams are rated for the 500kg point hoist load as well as accommodating additional chain hoist loads.

A pair of point hoist units. *Rear view of point hoists*

The grid has been kept very clear with all the powered rigging being overhead. The wire ropes to the multi-line across-stage bars also pass overhead and drop through conventional grid wells. The standard grille decking in each bay provides good access all around. The side areas of the grid above the galleries are concrete to provide a safe area for repairs and for working with small items which must never be taken loose onto the grid itself.

The Royal Theatre reviewed the scheme drawings and proposed the position in which the cyclorama passes across the stage. This does not give the full stage depth with the cyclorama in use but provides better lighting and allows significant storage of scenery upstage. The bars just downstage of it are affected by the curve and have had to be reduced in length but the upstage bars are the full width. The bar section is an aluminium extrusion produced by Triple E Ltd, known as "Unibeam". This extrusion has a range of track fittings and scenery hangers that can be fitted easily to allow simple and safe rigging of built scenery and cloths. Dimensions from centre are given on yellow tapes on the upstage and off-stage faces of the bars.

Stage Control System

The performance parameters of the bars and point hoists are given in the technical schedules in Chapter 16. Dave Ludlam joined the team during early days of the project to assist with the development of the power engineering and control systems. The special features of this stage control system include a fully distributed control structure with a dual redundant inter-connecting network. Each axis has its own 'embedded' drive and motion controller in a small cabinet above the hoist. All the connections between hoist and drive cabinet are via plugs and sockets and extension leads are provided to allow a drive cabinet to be 'cross-plugged' in the event of a failure. When cross-plugged the hoist number and settings are retained and it operates as if it were being driven by its original drive. Power is fed to the drive cabinets from overhead via industrial 'plug-in' busbars. The contractor was initially resistant to this idea from the consultant on cost grounds but later admitted that they had saved 'a fortune' on installation costs using this approach.

The multi-line hoists, motors and controllers on one side of motor room.

Winding drums at 400mm centres.

Point hoist wire rope passing through plastic guide in grid.

Rolling beams showing numbers.

Flying bars with position and load markers.

There are eight main control panels and four smaller portable rigger's control panels, one of which is wireless. Both styles of control panel run the same Graphical User Interface to minimise user training, the only difference being the number of joystick 'playbacks'. The system was developed largely along the lines specified and has a number of useful operational features. The wireless control panel has proved particularly useful for rigging point hoists in the grid.

CAT 180 control desk.

With multiple control panels and a duplicated central server containing all the system and show data we anticipate an extremely high level of availability for this system. Any faults that do occur can be quickly diagnosed using the system event log of all user actions, coupled with the real-time data from the built-in telemetry system which records signals such as motor speed, drive current and brake status for all active hoists. This data is then available to the manufacturer remotely for monitoring or diagnosis over an ISDN connection.

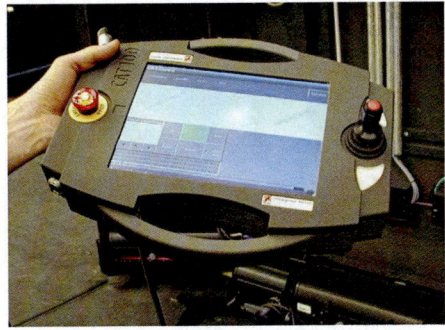

CAT 100 control desk.

Although the overstage lighting used by the Royal Theatre is expected, because of their repertoire, to be fairly constant in position, the facility of being able to hang lighting frames in any position was provided. This allows changes in position to be made and expedites fit-ups by visiting companies with their own lighting or those requiring special positions. Normally a set

Electrical connections to lighting frames.   *Overstage lighting frames.*

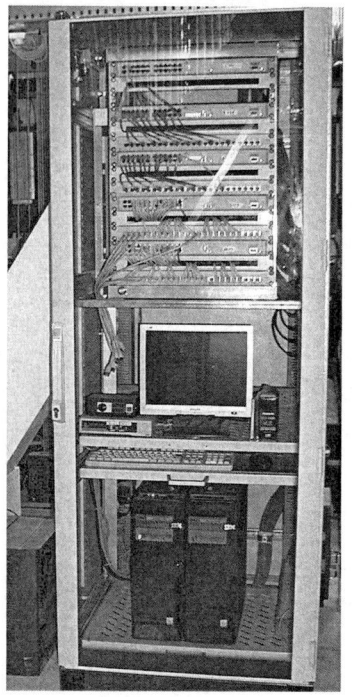

of six standard lighting frames are carried on four flying bars making a lighting rig with a length of about 18 metres and a total capacity of 3,200kg.

Power to the lighting frames is provided via the large powered windlasses which are formed into a control group with the four flying bars so that the whole set-up operates as one item. The windlasses, which are proprietary items, are driven upwards but are pulled downwards by the weight of the lighting frames against spring tensioning devices.

Overall the installations are very satisfactory but this was not achieved without a lot of careful thought and pressure by the consultants, and considerable co-operation from Waagner-Biro Stage Systems, Delstar Engineering, Priebe AS and the other smaller firms who contributed in different ways to the stage engineering installations. Getting both an environment in which the equipment will work properly and the right equipment for a project, not just what

Stage control rack in motor room.

was supplied last time, is a hard task. Areas where we had particularly good cooperation on technical issues were from the architects, who admitted this was an area in which they did not have any real experience, and from the structural engineering team at Rambøll. As we requested, the construction of the fly tower is concrete with steel trusses running up-downstage in the motor room, leaving the grid clear to be supported on slender hangers located accurately so as not to affect the placing of diverter pulleys. The team at Rambøll were also very helpful in accommodating some of the awkward load reactions which arose during the arrangement of small details, like those caused by the diversion of the wire ropes for the back-light frames to the hoist in the motor room.

It is strange that one of the biggest misunderstandings arose over the colour of the side and rear stages. The architects were keen to have a consistent colour scheme backstage and considered that this should continue into the stage and side stage areas. If one wall was to be black, they all had to be black! We felt otherwise and explained why we wanted light-coloured working areas with certain walls black, the rear of the safety curtain white and each of the off-stage faces of the dividing doors a different colour. After extensive trials of 'light colours' we ended up with all the working areas painted an acceptable shade and the safety curtain white, but totally failed to get walls likely to be seen in scene changes painted dark, or our colour identification on the doors. Our comments about, "Unless you do what is needed theatrically, the users will change it" have however been proven true as a major scene change on the

Rear of safety curtain painted white to improve working conditions on stage.

View from rear stage gallery of rear and rehearsal stages.

Copenhagen Opera House 155

stage wagons in the opening production of *Aida* necessitated the upstage wall of the side stage to be severely darkened! It also enabled the full potential of the stage wagons and elevators to be demonstrated successfully in the first production, although against the Consultants advice! A side stage wagon pushed another off-stage and when this additional piece was disconnected, the full side stage wagon with the temple setting was raised some 3 metres on the main stage elevators to reveal the tomb beneath for the last act.

The first 6 months of operations was not without the odd technical problem but these had minimum effect on performances. The theatre crew have declared themselves pleased to have had only an 11-minute delay in a performance in their first season. All theatres with extensive technical installations suffer the odd glitch, whether this is due to a computer refusing to boot up properly or the crew not having sufficient experience to be aware of everything that is going on. Technical operators have to be similar to airline pilots; the majority of cues can be done on autopilot (provided one keeps a clear eye on what is moving) but one needs sufficient skill to overcome the unexpected when it occurs. It is this skill that hopefully will soon be fully developed.

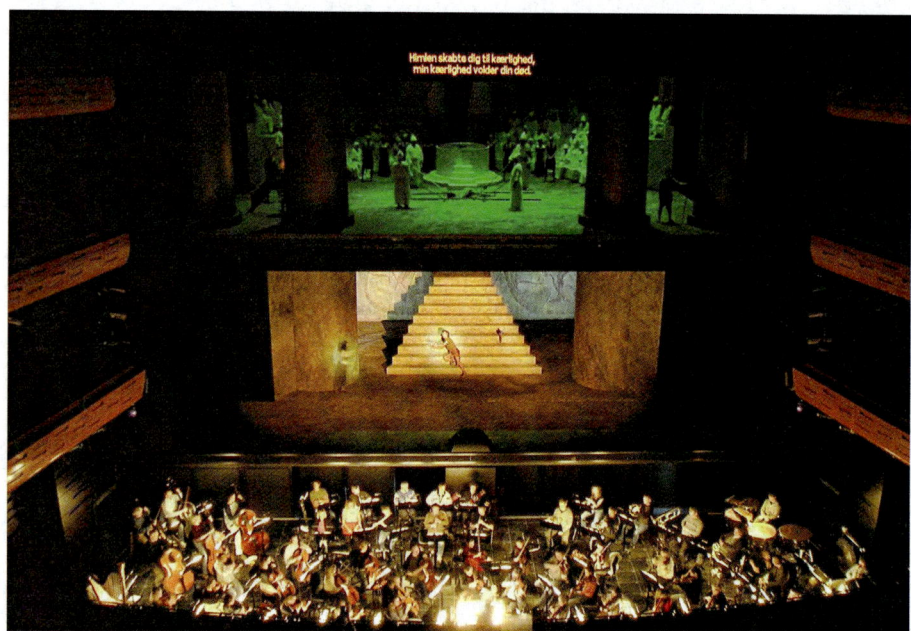

The final tomb scene in Aida played on two levels.

The final tomb scene in Aida played on two levels.

Chief electrician Rene Conradi with the grandMA lighting control console.

Part of the 450-plus line-up of Robert Juliat luminaires.

10 STAGE LIGHTING IN OPERAEN
John Whitaker, Richard Brett

One of the world's leading lighting designers, with a tremendous background in lighting opera and ballet, as well as having been Lighting Consultant to the Royal Opera House, Covent Garden, works with Theatreplan on the concepts of the stage lighting schemes for major theatres and opera houses. John B Read developed the scheme for the Gran Teatre del Liceu in Barcelona and also came on board in Copenhagen to establish the scale and form of the stage lighting installation for one of the first major opera houses to be looking at 21st century technology.

John had lit performances by the Royal Danish Ballet many years previously at the Royal Theatre in Copenhagen but now examined anew the lighting facilities and layouts that he believed would be appropriate for this opera and ballet house which was scheduled to work in fairly heavy repertoire. In this he drew on his extensive experience, particularly in the way that the stage lighting rig in the Royal Opera House, which had come into service late in 1999, was working. He also took into account the special requirements of the Royal Theatre, especially in relation to their existing working practices. Together with John Whitaker and Richard Brett, the lighting scheme was reviewed with the lighting personnel at the Royal Theatre in a couple of meetings and the principles of the required layouts, numbers and sizes of circuits were generally agreed.

John Whitaker was in charge of the stage lighting and work lighting installations for the new opera for Theatreplan and he brought in Mike Atkinson who had been trialling the use of distributed dimming in the National Theatre in London. Mike had a large involvement with the control network infrastructure and assisted with drafting some of the Employer's Requirements. One of the major concerns, and one which had caused difficulties in the Royal Opera House, was the number of circuits which modern lighting requires over stage. This had led to special 'cable bridges' being hung just under the grid above the lighting battens in order to handle the large numbers of multi-core cables. Apart from the physical difficulty of handling the quantities of connections, the multi-core cables are extremely heavy and cannot easily be relocated.

Multicore cable feeds in the Royal Opera House.

One of the requirements in Copenhagen was that the lighting frames should be able to be hung wherever needed for a season: this flexibility wasn't seen as being a production change but was to be available so that the stage could accommodate a dance season or a musical in which a different overstage rig was required.

The principle of distributed dimming meant that if the dimmers could be of a type that could be mounted with the luminaires on the lighting frames over stage, then the problem was reduced to feeding electrical power to the lighting frames, not handling a very large number of individual circuits. Consideration of electrical engineering principles also revealed the excessive amount of copper that often had to be installed in these multi-cores. By using sine-wave dimmers overstage the power factor of the dimmers improves and the cables feeding the power to the dimmers become much more efficient. This was to be the basis of one of the major developments in the stage lighting system.

The principle appeared sound but new principles are not always trusted in the theatre where practice makes perfect – if it's been done before and it works then you can probably trust it! The benefits of feeding raw power down to the lighting frames and then providing compact sine-wave dimmers, switched circuits and un-switched circuits on the lighting frames using units that can be plugged up as required appeared considerable in terms of flexibility and efficiency. Mike had already completed an installation of sine-wave dimmers in the Lyttelton Theatre in the National Theatre building in London and this had indicated a trouble-free existence. Even the fear of the MCBs tripping overstage during a show was overcome when remote resetting of these was demonstrated. So the search was on for a suitable method of getting power down to the lighting frames.

A number of major UK theatres have had various forms of lighting windlasses over the years and these came back in a new form; a development of a proprietary power windlass as used on container cranes on docks, in mining and many other industrial applications. A Danish company, Cavotech, offered a unit that could provide three 3-phase 60A cables on each windlass with two CAT-6 cables incorporated in each power cable, giving a total of six CAT-6 circuits altogether. The total power of 180A 3-phase would be used at a power-factor of about 1 reducing losses in the cables very significantly.

The windlasses are mounted on the gallery immediately below the grid and are arranged to be driven as part of the group of hoists which are carrying the lighting frames. They are powered when raising but operate with a slipping clutch on the way down. The overall installation is very tidy and does not obstruct the grid or the overstage space to any degree. The cables can be disconnected from the lighting frames and wound up to their diverter pulleys so that these can be brought inboard of the gallery and moved up or down stage to a new position. The lighting frames themselves can be lowered into trolleys and detached from the flying bars so that these too can be repositioned or replaced with other preset lighting frames. Although this is not a frequent operation the lighting crew have taken to these arrangements and are very enthusiastic for the system and its flexibility. Following this installation the only conclusions the consultants will consider on the next project are the ways to make the frame structure more adaptable so as to more easily accommodate a larger range of luminaires and a different attachment system which will allow the tilt of the frames to be corrected by relative motion of the flying bars.

Elsewhere in the building the stage lighting infrastructure is rather more conventional. There are three dimmer rooms or locations for the mainstage; a set of dimmer racks in the hoist motor room which is above the grid, a dimmer room to the side of the auditorium and a further set of racks just under stage. The above-grid space is thinly populated as it was planned before the over stage

Lighting power windlasses on windlass gallery just below grid.

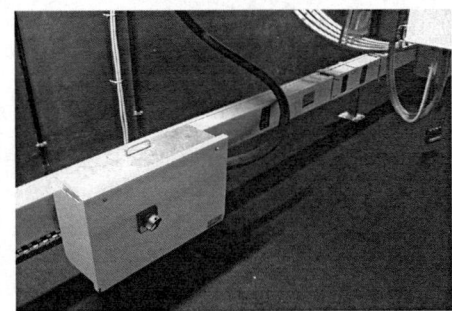

200A 3-phase bus-bar plug-in connection for windlass.

Lighting frames hanging on four flying bars.

sine-wave dimmer arrangement was finalised and now these dimmers only feed the opera portal and galleries within the fly tower.

The auditorium dimmer room handles the circuits in the ceiling openings, on the technical gallery and on the balcony fronts and beneath the tiers right round to the near proscenium positions. The under stage dimmers feed the outlets at stage level, in the dip traps, those under stage and in the orchestra pit.

Lighting frames showing cyc lighting on end.

This arrangement was created to reduce the lengths of sub-circuits in order to minimise volt-drop. In this area a small cost-saving was made by wiring some circuits in the dip traps in parallel with those in the main upstage and downstage outlet panels: elsewhere all the circuits are unique and directly addressable by channel. They are all ETC

Power panels and dimmer racks in motor room above the grid.

Dimmer racks in services area below stage.

Interior of a production lighting outlet box.

Production lighting outlets in dip-trap in compensator elevator.

Production lighting wiring in part of the under stage.

Sensor dimmers rated at 5kW and 3kW. The sine-wave dimmers have a feature which will appeal to many technicians; by pressing a recessed button two 3kW dimmers become a 5kW circuit, controlled as the lower number of the pair of dimmers.

The auditorium is provided with some excellent lighting positions although the original intention of having conventional lighting bridges was overtaken

Lighting gallery in use.

by the various alternative forms of ceiling examined by the architect, acoustician and client before deciding on the convex form of ceiling with minimum openings.

The slots are designed to accommodate a number of luminaires but the fire-protection on the suspensions supporting the ceiling restricted the access to these positions to such a degree that luminaires with remotely-controlled yokes were finally mounted in each of the sixteen openings. These yokes were made by Brother, Brother & Sons in Denmark towards the end of the project. There are also very accessible and well-sited lighting positions all around a fifth level

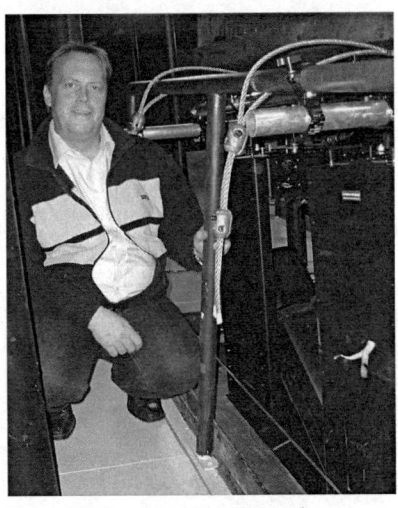

Søren Nylin demonstrating the restricted access in the roof void.

Copenhagen Opera House 165

Convex ceiling plane from below showing the lighting slots.

above the auditorium tiers and on the technical gallery (the fourth tier) which make the limited ceiling openings an acceptable solution.

Lower frontal lighting is provided by metal arms which hinge out of some of the slotted openings in the balcony fronts to support lights or other additional equipment. Also a main and a secondary lighting position on the acoustic reflector near the proscenium provide the appropriate angles and a near top light position for lighting downstage in the portal zone. Side lighting is fully provided by the luminaires on the side booms and under the tiers. A large sound-proof room on the centre line at the rear

Lighting equipment just visible on the fourth tier, the technical gallery.

Hinged luminaire brackets folded away in balcony front.

Hinged luminaire brackets partially extended.

Hinged luminaire brackets extended for use.

Lighting mounted under the side balconies and on a near-stage boom.

of the auditorium on the highest level has five angled windows and accommodates up to four follow spots.

In addition to the lighting frames overstage, the opera portal is fully provided with side lighting on the tormentor towers and on a two level bridge. Although designed to minimum dimensions so as not to push any settings further upstage than necessary, there is adequate space for the equipment and access.

Auditorium from rear stage showing the followspot room.

Tormentor tower showing overhead outlets.

Portal lighting bridge.

Portal lighting bridge special fitting detail.

The power distribution was developed from the system installed at the Royal Opera House in London. Main power supplies are run to locations around the stage, fly tower, grid and roof void and including the dimmer locations. These provide a local source of power everywhere, either by direct wiring or from sockets on the power panel or via sub-circuits to uncontrolled outlets in the vicinity. These can be used for general purposes, additional lighting or stage machinery. Each power panel incorporates contactors for non-dim circuits and also for the control of work lights in the area, the contactors being fed by Ethernet and DMX signals. Power outlets range, depending on the location and anticipated use, from 400A 3-phase on stage for additional dimmer racks for a touring production with its own rig, down to 16A and 10A circuits single-phase.

The work light system is very comprehensive and includes both bright white

Example of power panel wiring in progress.

One of the smaller power panels ready for wiring.

lights for fit-up conditions and controlled lower-intensity lights for use backstage in performances and rehearsals. Switching of individual circuits and to change the status of the system is provided by touch screen panels in the lighting control room and in each downstage corner. Local push buttons which are illuminated when the fit-up lights can be operated are mounted at most access points to the stage, galleries, grid, under stage and orchestra pit.

Denmark has a number of specific electrical regulations which did cause both the overseas consultants and contractors some grief: one of these was the unacceptability of the Schuko two-pin connector even within locked cabinets with only authorised access. Another was the installation of special outlets for computing equipment although most of the portable computers used appeared to be wired with conventional plugs. Aluminium cables were selected on economic grounds by the electrical consultants, Rambøll AS, and were very generously sized in accordance with, it appeared later, some future Danish regulations. The limited bending radius and size of these cables required an additional chamber to be fitted to many power

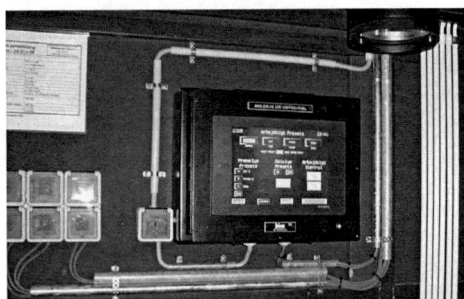

Work-light control panel on stage.

Rear fly tower galleries lit in blues.

ETC Sensor racks being wired.

panels and for higher fault-level switchgear to be provided than was envisaged at the start of the project, potentially neutralising some of the savings. Additional termination chambers also had to be fitted to the ETC Sensor dimmer cabinets in order to accommodate the double-insulated cables used in a tray installation.

There were also difficulties in co-ordinating the services within the fly tower. Despite establishing two service cores at the rear of the stage behind the fly tower, one with a fly tower lift and each with staircases and duct, pipe and rising cable ducts, the engineers later had to ask that a major electrical busbar, some of their air ducts and other services be run within the tower. This led to local areas where there are slight obstructions, but generally the galleries are spacious and easy to access and to work on.

The lower galleries incorporate a DIN lighting rail (two back to back channels) into which are mounted individual pipe sockets with a clamping screw as used by the Royal Theatre for their main lighting fixtures. There are also lighting pipes above and below the DIN rail as Theatreplan strongly recommended, despite the observation that the lighting crew wouldn't use the lower pipe.

As anticipated the lower position often achieves the critical position needed by lighting designers and so the mesh safety screens do come off! The upper galleries all have lighting rails and the side galleries have facilities for cleats and tie-offs. The galleries are all floored with fire-proofed plywood and covered with a short-tuft industrial carpet to minimise noise and to create a practical working environment.

A clear gallery below the windlass level.

The power panels provide the hubs of the control infrastructure. A comprehensive distribution of Ethernet signals to each power panel and each major production lighting outlet box links to a network hub or node providing a local feed of DMX which is distributed as required for stage lighting and remote luminaire control, and used in the power panels for the control of the work lighting. The full control system, network, desk and peripherals are described in the next chapter. There was very good co-operation between the dimmer supplier, ETC, who handled both their own and the IES sine-wave dimmers on this project, and MA Lighting. ETC even extended to MA Lighting permission to incorporate ETC's software, ETCNet2, in the control desk to drive the dimmers.

Lighting equipment rigged above and below rail.

Light gallery showing under rail positions.

The lighting control room is located at the back of the first tier next to a scenic projection room on the auditorium centre line. Both these rooms offer a very

Robert Juliat luminaires on brackets to allow steep down lighting angles.

good view of the stage. In line with Theatreplan's practice where there is a professional client, the selection of the control desk, luminaires and accessories was largely handled by Søren Nylin, a lighting designer with the Royal Theatre. Søren was seconded to the main building contractor E Pihl and Søn AS to act as technical liaison and provided great help and support, and even translations when things got sticky! This was another example of a project being run correctly, with the specialist consultants being able to develop their designs and introduce new approaches, while collaborating with a practical technical person with authority to make decisions for the user's team.

Side lighting tower in position.

Lighting frames hanging on stage.

11 LIGHTING CONTROL AND NETWORKING Ulrich Kunkel

It does not happen very often that an Opera House is built from virtually nothing to create a new landmark of a cultural and artistic level that none other has achieved before, but that it also reaches architectural and technical standards that will certainly not easily be gained by any other theatre in the world. And always must be kept in mind – firstly, that this was a gift to the people of Denmark so that they could come, see and enjoy opera, ballet and other productions in perfect conditions. And secondly, that there are hundreds of technicians and engineers who consider themselves proud to have been a member of that great team which made the whole project possible!

My own roots are in theatre as I started my career in the lighting industry some twenty years ago working as a volunteer in one of Germany's larger opera houses in Kassel. Since then I have been involved in the refurbishment of nearly a dozen theatres worldwide, but none of these projects ever reached the scale of the Copenhagen's "Operaen" which in many ways is the most unique modern opera house in the world.

Long before the building of the opera actually started, news about this upcoming milestone in theatre technology was spreading around the market and every manufacturer of lighting and control gear was keen to participate in this project. The plan to build a new opera house in a city which already had a large and renowned opera house was so unusual that there was expectation that the specification of the lighting systems for this building were going to be particularly interesting. Not only would the resulting installations have to meet the scale of the actual building and its individual architecture and extensive facilities, but also the whole world would have an eye on the technical standards involved in this project, which were expected to set a standard for any future installations in the theatre industry throughout Europe.

A unique feature of the planning phase on this project was that to accommodate the scale of the lighting systems, these were split into separate major parts right from the beginning. For the dimming installations, electrical power engineering, control infrastructure and power distribution, the Theatreplan team under John Whitaker was responsible. John worked with colleagues Mike Atkinson and Dave Ludlam on the control and power aspects of the planning and specifications. The other equipment which required a more artistic and operational preference, like the actual lighting control desk and the various spotlights and automated fixtures, was passed to the Royal (Kongelige) Theatre to make the final decisions about, within the appropriate budget. This was handled by Søren Nylin of the lighting department of the Kongelige Teater in Copenhagen so that the users could maintain a direct influence over actual selection of those parts of the system that effectively interface with the control and dimming infrastructure. Søren had been seconded to the Managing Contractor, E Pihl & Søn, to provide liaison between Pihl, the theatre consultants and the Kongelige Teater. In this way, the dimming system, the control infrastructure, the lighting control system and the actual lighting fixtures and luminaires formed many separate tenders, which led to independent contracts or purchase orders for the various parts. This allowed a wide selection of equipment to be purchased to fulfil the needs of the project. My first contact with this millennium project was when my employer at that time received an invitation to submit a quotation for the specified dimming system for the new Copenhagen Operaen, which was named "The Opera Project in Copenhagen" at that stage.

Dimmers and Their Future

Having taken a first look at the specification for the dimmer and distribution system it was immediately clear to me that this was going to be one of the best engineered and well thought-through systems I had ever seen. Instead of following the easy way and putting the system specification in the hands of one manufacturer only (which sometimes happens as dimmers are known to be the most boring but essential parts of any theatre lighting installation), this system suddenly came up with some new and fresh ideas. This really made it enjoyable to work out solutions to the detailed requirements given, using known products that we could source.

Unlike other installations where the dimmer rooms, which are required in most theatre lighting systems to control the intensity of the still-dominant tungsten spot lights, are centralised in one single room (which historically used to be somewhere in the basement), this scheme made provision for four decentralised dimmer rooms. This helped to split the number of dimmer circuits into smaller groups and moved them closer to the actual luminaires. In a large theatre building like an opera house this helps to save money on the actual

Lighting frames with sine-wave dimmers and switching units mounted within them.

electrical installation as the load cable lengths are kept as short as possible. Also cable core diameters can be reduced as the expected voltage drop to the luminaires is not going to be as critical as if all the cabling was run out of the basement of what is effectively a 14 storey building.

Something even more unusual was the idea to move some of the dimmers even closer than normal to the actual loads they controlled. So the plan put forward by Theatreplan was to mount nearly a third of all the dimmer circuits for this opera house directly on the five suspended lighting bridges within the fly tower. This principle is not new but, until now, the technology of dimmers had not developed far enough to allow a system of this type to be installed in practice. These dimmers had to be nearly acoustically noiseless as they were going to be installed as close as any other part of the system to the live stage. They also had to fulfil mandatory standards for safety and electromagnetic compliance. The only possible solution to comply with these parameters and the specification was the use of so-called 'sine-wave' dimming technology, which is actually based on a high-frequency pulse-width-modulation system.

Any system which is built on decentralised placement of electrical switchgear like the dimmer system for the Copenhagen Opera needs to incorporate an extensive fault detection and feedback system otherwise it will never survive the practical needs of daily theatre and show operations. So full dimmer feedback and remote configuration and service was part of the tender right from the beginning, although the way it was to be implemented was left fairly open in the specification. This was finalised in more detail when the actual system was ordered. But we will come to that later.

The possible ban on electrical switchgear using phase-switching technology from use in official buildings in the foreseeable future by the standards office of the European Community was anticipated, so the dimmer cabinets had to be able to be retrofitted with modules using sine-wave technology if this were ever to apply to the Copenhagen opera house.

The contractual part of the dimming system also included all local connectors and connection boxes on stage and in other lighting positions to provide the outlets for the dedicated luminaires and lighting fixtures. This also included local power distribution units for any lighting or other equipment in use on the stage, including any which requires non-dimmed mains power. At the time when the order for the dimming system was placed, more than 1,000 fixed and installed dimmer circuits were specified for use in the four dimmer rooms. Three of these dimmer rooms were for the main stage and the fourth for the studio stage. In addition 350 distributed dimmers, plus another 120 non-dim circuits, all to be installed on the five suspended lighting bridges

ETC Sensor dimmer racks.

on main stage, were included in the final specification. These circuits had to be wired up to over 200 individually-tailored production lighting boxes within the main stage and the studio stage. The studio stage later got the name "Takelloftet", called after the old place next to the opera where masts and rigging for sailing ships were built in the past. An additional 30 power panels around both stages ensure that there will be enough mains power and different types of connection for future lighting and stage engineering applications which are still not thought of yet!

The Key to Flexibility – Data Distribution

Another and most important part of the dimmer and power distribution contract included in the specification was the desired data distribution system on both stages. It was intended to create a most future-proof distribution network which would be suitable for all existing and upcoming communication protocols for lighting applications. Most lighting fixtures still use DMX 512 as the one and only common control signal, but basing a new design of control network on this signal, which has not changed in speed or capacity since its introduction in 1986, would not have been the right choice for the world's most sophisticated opera house. Unfortunately the long expected new upcoming standard ACN (which stands for "architecture for control networks") has not left the ESTA task group and has, even today, not reached more than the fourth stage of public review.

So with the agreement of the Kongelige Teater, led by Søren Nylin, the decision was made to plan and install a sophisticated network distribution system. This was to be capable of running the currently-used manufacturer-specific protocols and the right platform for ACN, and was to allow a future changeover of the complete system without any rework or additional hardware installation. All manufacturers of dimmers

Main data distribution rack and lighting control servers.

and lighting control gear have to commit themselves to a possible future implementation of ACN in their products as soon as the protocol is released. It was never intended to ban DMX from the opera as it is the only existing link to most dimmers, moving lights and other automated fixtures. In fact the way the distribution of DMX was designed already follows the basic ideas of the ACN outline. So some 120 network nodes which convert a given EtherNet protocol back into DMX 512 were designed into the system and these are placed in designated production lighting boxes. Also all dimmers had to be controlled by direct EtherNet input which was also planned to be used as the remote configuration and feedback protocol.

But how were we to design a distribution network for a building, the routing dimensions of which easily exceed those of any other opera in the world? Because of the technical limitations of an EtherNet system based on copper wires where cable runs need to be kept below 100 metres, it was quite obvious that fibre-optic systems needed to be installed. Starting from the lighting control room, all three dimmer rooms and both windlass galleries of the main stage were linked together on EtherNet "backbones" each equipped with 1Gb EtherNet uplinks using fibre optical cables. The studio stage was also linked into this network to allow easy remote network monitoring and software updates. On all these junction points EtherNet distribution racks were provided from which the decentralised local network nodes, like lighting control equipment, EtherNet-to-DMX nodes, dimmer racks and the whole working light control system were wired on standard CAT 6 cables to the main network. For additional security the fibre-optic data lines were run in redundant pairs to avoid any downtime of the network or parts of the network if mechanical damage or other defect occurs to the actual fibre-optic cable or connectors.

A total of seven data distribution cabinets are installed, each containing network switches to receive data on the fibre-optic link to the control room and to convert this into 10/100Mb 'Fast EtherNet' links to the local equipment. Both racks in the control rooms of the main stage and the studio stage additionally contain an uninterruptible power supply unit to avoid any downtime of the whole network or data loss caused by possible mains supply failures.

If ACN had been available at the time of installation the whole network distribution would have been far more straightforward as all of the proposed equipment would have happily coexisted on the same network backbone. But that would have been too easy...

So unfortunately each of the major two parts of the lighting system – control and dimming – ended up using its own manufacturer-specific network protocol and there were concerns that these might each interfere with its counterpart in the system. Therefore it was decided that for all major parts of the lighting system (dimming system, control system and wireless network for remote control) separate routes from each distribution rack to the main control room had to be installed. In actuality this required the cabling and network equipment for the EtherNet backbone to be multiplied by three – with the given expectation that two of these parts would be made redundant as soon as ACN becomes available for all the installed components. This can be compared with a world where all the systems are working fine independently, but none of it is really 'speaking' to the other parts. Another show stopper in this phase of the planning was the fact that the specification for the designated control system was not at the time finally published and the parts of the dimming and working light control system which had already been tendered had to be as open as possible to allow interfacing with all other kinds of control protocols – including DMX.

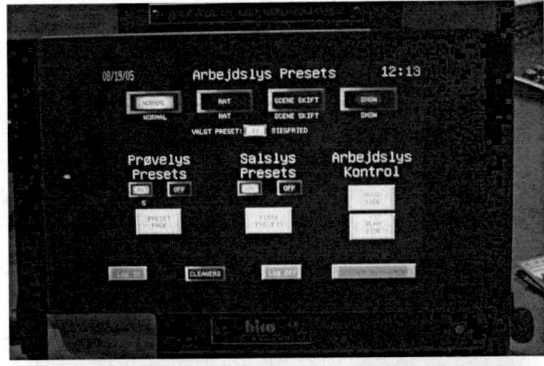
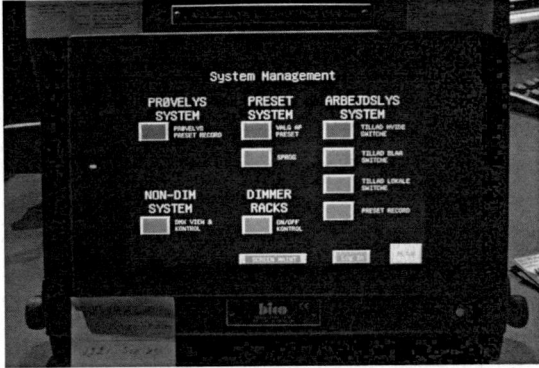
Working light control panels.

After the review of all received quotations by Theatreplan, the decision was made to place the order for the dimming and data distribution system with Electronic Theatre Controls (ETC) who at that time was the only company able to supply all the specified technology through one contractor. ETC was represented by Bico Lighting in Denmark who had Søren Jørgensen in the role of project leader for this part of the system.

Who Takes Control?

The story of the next major part on the lighting system of the Copenhagen Opera – the lighting control desk and associated facilities – started a lot differently than the tender for the dimmers and control infrastructure. The dimming system with all its cabinets, network equipment and power distribution boxes required a detailed tender document which nearly filled a complete binder, whereas the lighting control equipment was specified in a spread sheet format on only a few pages.

This was made possible by the fact that only a few manufacturers of lighting control equipment have gone down the route of using the network as an extensive communication platform for all the relevant data affecting the lighting, and have not just created a repackaging for DMX data.

When the staff of the lighting department of the Kongelige Teater with Søren Nylin as their spokesman started to search in their imaginations for a future-proof lighting control system it became quite clear that none of the currently available systems on the market would provide all the facilities they identified. So it was most important that the control system to fulfil their requirements must be able to 'grow' in any new direction in which the lighting industry may decide the control philosophy and the related protocols were going to go. Even the introduction of ACN would be a major task for that system even if that protocol was to be available on the day the opera was to be commissioned. The more these technologically-based arguments were collated, the more also the list of required operational features grew. This was very much focused on the actual equipment which was planned to be controlled by the designated system. The impressive number of dimmers was only one aspect of the expected workload for the control system which also had to control various types of moving lights in large quantities, motorised yokes for theatrical luminaires with high precision position detection, Fresnel spots with discharge lamps also mounted in motorised yokes and additionally equipped with remotely controlled barndoors, and some hundreds of colour scrollers in various sizes. In fact only a third of all the required DMX circuits would be used for conventional dimmers and luminaires; all the rest would be required by all that fancy equipment just listed!

Many systems currently available would cope with this kind of workload but only a few will respect the fact that a board operator in an opera house could be easily overloaded in a lighting rehearsal. This is a time when there are not many auxiliary devices, in addition to the main control system, available

grandMA: full size console in the lighting control room.

to share that workload with the right people in the lighting department simultaneously. The right system for the opera really needed to be a so-called multi-user system which in any case is always very much software based. So it was not very surprising that the lighting control system finally identified was the one with the largest balance between technical capabilities, network implementation and operational features – and one which was not typically a theatrical console.

With their 'grandMA' lighting console range, the German manufacturer MA Lighting introduced a rather unusual control system quite a while ago. Originally aimed towards the entertainment market with big shows and a great number of moving lights, the MA console has more and more been developed in theatrical directions. This is in many ways the responsibility of one of the mental fathers of 'grandMA' – the well known Thomas Brockmann - himself a native Danish citizen. So by helping his friend Søren Nylin to solve his complex requirements for a really versatile theatrical lighting control desk one could have said he helped grandMA to be brought home again!

The specification for the lighting control system just simply described the required hardware components and operational features of a grandMA system suitable for the size of an opera like the Copenhagen Operaen and allowed the bidder to offer his own system as far as he could, and also fulfil the operational features that are offered by a system like this.

Finally the order was placed with Gobo Lighting, the Copenhagen representative of MA Lighting, where Thomas Riishøj took over the responsibility as project leader. Also at that time my own practical involvement in the opera project started as a freelance engineer and network specialist for the implementation of the control system into the already installed infrastructure.

Bringing Some Worlds Together

When in the past a lighting control desk needed to be linked to a dimmer system this would not have been a major issue – especially since DMX 512 was commonly used by nearly all manufacturers. But that was not the situation on this project. On both sides we had most sophisticated theatrical lighting systems – on one, the dimmers with an extensive communication network, and on the other, the lighting control with a most versatile network functionality. But as ACN was still out of sight and both ends were using their own propriety network protocol where the only common thing seemed to be the actual network cable connector, DMX seemed to be the only way these systems could communicate with each other.

And so the first system design was prepared. From the consoles' network some processing nodes produce eight(!) DMX output lines which were then fed into some input network nodes on the dimmer side which were converting the DMX signal back into a network protocol which the dimmer system and all the decentralised output nodes could understand. Though this meant a clear separation between both systems and the whole installation worked well right from the beginning, none of the involved parties really liked that solution. The one who really hated it and felt his ideas about ACN were being postponed forever was Søren Nylin – and he was right. Despite the fact that the dimmers were dimming and the moving lights were moving, the system itself was felt to be in a dead end and soon some delay problems were discovered. With its total of eight DMX universes, which equal more than 4,000 control channels, the 'grandMA' desk could send so many changed values at one

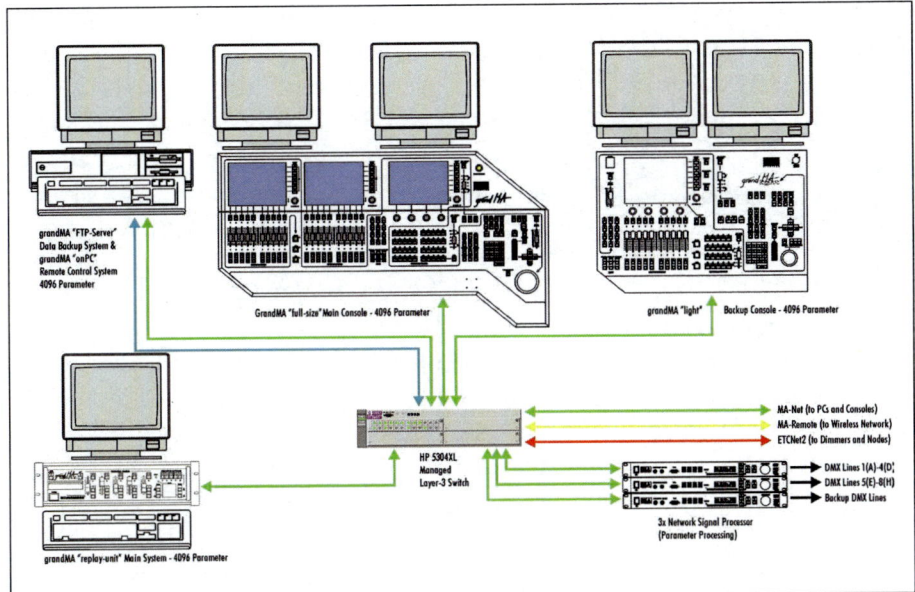

Main stage control schematic.

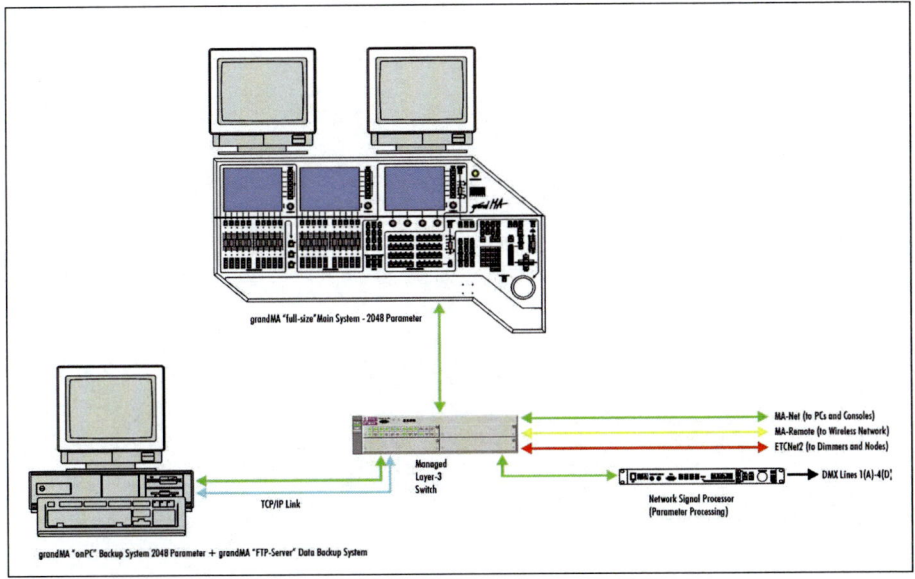

Studio stage control schematic.

Copenhagen Opera House 183

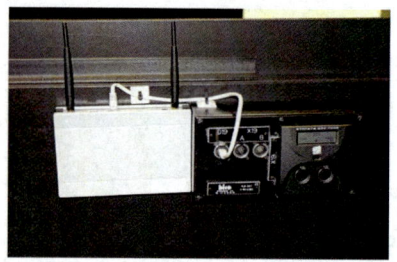

Wireless LAN node.

time (worst case when all 1,500 dimmers were dialled up and down quite rapidly) that the receiving ETCNet2 nodes on the other end of the DMX lines had too much to do to get those changes translated into network traffic. On stage there seemed to be a visible delay in the response of some dimmers which were still adjusting the changes even when the console was already back in a static lighting cue.

So how to get that problem fixed? Very simple – even when it was a hard work to get everybody involved to be convinced by the necessity of the required steps. First we needed to find a common network protocol for both systems – without reinventing the wheel and always keeping in mind that ACN might change the system in the future anyway. So as all the dimmers were already listening to ETCNet2 via EtherNet, why not just add this protocol to the consoles' multi-protocol stack? This sounds easy but meant hard work for all parties. First of all, two sometimes competing companies needed to talk to each other and needed to start exchanging the necessary information to enable the required R&D processes to be started. As both protocols 'MA-Net' and

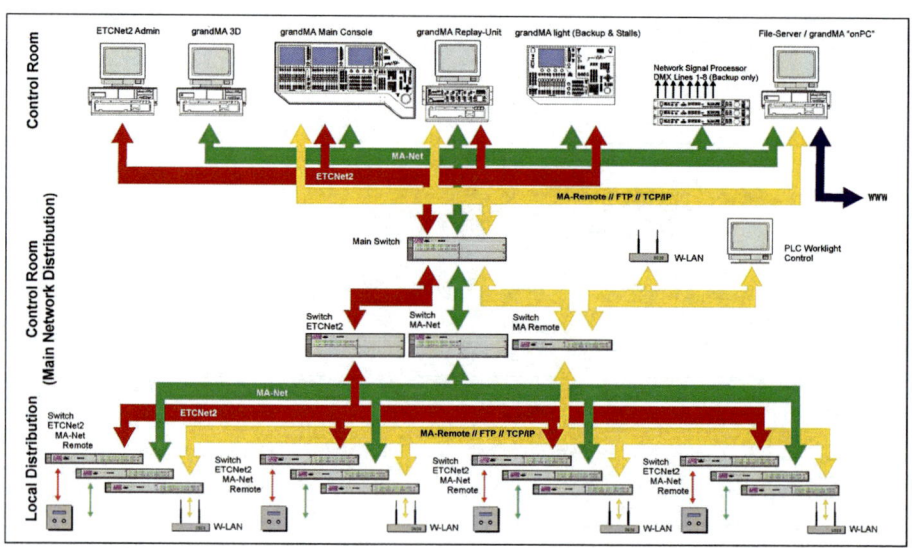

Main stage control data connectivity.

'ETCNet2' are non-public and not 'open source' this required an agreement from both sides. But finally everybody was sure that the future release and availability of ACN will make agreements like this unnecessary – so why not support maybe the most important customer in a major opera house at that time with a bit of the future, and do it now?

So after some weeks of development the first 'grandMA' software was finally talking ETCNet2 to the Sensor dimmers. I have to say we all felt like little pioneers when these first few luminaires pointing in the orchestra pit suddenly dimmed up smoothly and with no more visible delays in response to the control changes. The two network trees 'MA-Net' and 'ETCNet2' were now just simply linked together and information flowed from one into the other segment easily. But unfortunately this started some new problems which helped all of us to discover the core nature of ACN before it was ever released.

Multi-User Really Means Many, Many Operators

Before we come back to these new discoveries, let me just explain some more details of the components in the control parts of the lighting system.

One main idea of the Kongelige Teater's crew was to allow the lighting technicians on stage to dial up their own channels for focusing without keeping the main board operator busy all the time. Many lighting control system offer a hand held remote but here the requirements were even more specific. Up to six wireless remotes, plus another two for the "Takelloftet", were to be able to work independently of each other and this even when the main console is switched off or no operator is available. To achieve this kind of functionality, a lighting playback server (called a replay unit) was planned into the system. This was basically a full lighting console in a box, but without a lot of faders, knobs or screens. This unit was mounted in an equipment rack in another room, next to where the lighting consoles were placed, and therefore performs as a real backup system, being operational even when the main control was unavailable or the room was locked. The replay unit had to run day and night and also had to keep record copies of all shows used and programmed by the main system. To protect against data loss, a second file server from which all the consoles and lighting PCs can read data, keeps copies of all versions of the shows that have ever been used in the theatre.

The hand-held remote used by the technicians is like a pocket PC with some dedicated software which can log onto this lighting playback server at any time (if not prohibited by the main console). The technician can thus start working with his 'own' lights without disturbing the work of any of the board operators. This is also extremely useful during lighting rehearsal where the operator is normally quite busy and does not like other devices interfering with 'his' lights.

To make this hand-held control idea come true, an extensive wireless network had to be installed with WLAN coverage of all main lighting positions. For the main stage this was achieved by a total of eight wireless access points; four more were installed for the studio stage. As many of the network devices had to placed in some very odd positions, the use of PoE, 'Power over EtherNet' technology, where the supply voltage for a device was fed through the data cable itself, was extremely helpful. All the EtherNet to DMX network nodes were remotely powered by the same system.

The main lighting control system simply consists of one 'grandMA:full-size' console, which is most of the time doing its job nearly alone, as its fully-redundant backup console – a 'grandMA:light' is most of the time used on stage or in the auditorium for rehearsals. The absence of the backup desk is actually no problem as the required security is also provided by the lighting playback server. This can be comfortably operated and controlled from a PC version of the 'grandMA' software, also installed on the data backup server but fully accessible from a keyboard, mouse and monitor next to the main console.

With two notebook computers utilising 'grandma:onPC' software on-line on the network for rehearsals and especially working off-line for editing from the office, the lighting managers have gained some more freedom in the way they work. The same software is also used on two tablet PCs (one on stage right and one on the galleries) which offer some more comfort in operating the lighting system than the pocket PC remotes, even when the main console is off-line.

The only part of the whole lighting system on the main stage not controlled by the stage lighting console network, is the house lighting system in the auditorium. This consists of over 1,000 channels of LED fixtures and low voltage beamlights with a fibre optic lighting system, all of which was designed by consultants Speirs & Major from the UK. This uses an ETC 'Emphasis' as a control system to play back some predefined cues. Nevertheless this system also uses the ETCNet2 network for data distribution.

With all these components together talking on the same network (especially since the link between the 'MA-Net' and 'ETCNet2' parts were installed) we experienced some strange effects on some network nodes as well as on the control systems. Both 'ETCNet2' and 'MA-Net' are using the so-called 'multicast' transmission of data. This is received by virtually all the nodes and components on the network which results in a lot of network traffic and we found that we really needed to keep some parts of the network free from unnecessary traffic to ensure the full performance of the connected nodes. The wireless network part especially was totally overloaded with all the dimmer control and console information and needed to be filtered from that traffic to keep the performance of the wireless remotes high.

To solve this traffic overload in some parts of the network – which was already identified as one possible problem with ACN in the future (ACN is also based on 'multicast' communication) – a 'layer 3' manageable network switch was installed to handle the link between 'MA-Net', 'ETCNet2' and the wireless network. This switch also blocks any traffic from one part to another part of the system if, by mistake, a wrong network connector was used on stage to connect a control desk or a DMX output node. Since the switch was installed and finally configured, no further problems have been experienced and the system works as reliably as when DMX was the only link between both worlds.

The complete lighting rig of Operaen.

A Hope for Some More Nights at the Opera
During the time the various systems were being installed at the Operaen in Copenhagen, some most valuable experience was gained about using some of the latest technology from manufacturers from all over the world and I really had one of the greatest times in my life. Not only was I lost more than once in a building that, with its uncountable numbers of stairways and elevators, sometimes behaves like the pyramids of Gizeh when trying to find your way out, but I am really proud to have been part of that real international family of consultants, technicians and specialists which helped to get everything finished in time to give Denmark undoubtedly the most admirable theatre building ever – and hopefully not only from an engineer's point of view.

12. ARCHITECTURAL LIGHTING OF OPERAEN Jonathan Speirs, Keith Bradshaw

Introduction

The lighting design for any opera house should be an intrinsic part of the image and experience of the building, where the glamour and drama of the building adds to the enjoyment of the opera-goer. The sparkle of a chandelier, the excitement as houselights extinguish are key parts of the expectation of an opera house. To architectural lighting designers an opera house sets a series of technical and aesthetic challenges. The lighting design must enhance the experience of the opera-goer both visually and psychologically.

We were appointed in 2002 to join the team to design the architectural lighting for the new Opera House. This fast track project demanded a strong focus and attention to detail to serve an informed and demanding client who expected only the best from his team of consultants. In terms of an architectural design and concept, the project demanded integration of the lighting design into the building, with luminaires concealed from view allowing the architecture to appear elegantly luminous.

Our commission included the exterior of the building, the main foyers, the main auditorium and the orchestra rehearsal room. We also gave secondary assistance, and our opinion on proposals, to the architectural team on the architectural lighting design in the studio stage, the staff restaurant and rehearsal areas.

We conceived this building's image as being one of a lantern; the inner areas of the foyers acting as a source, attracting one's eye inside the space. The public areas of opera houses are inherently spaces for people to see and be seen in and our goal was to try and enhance this by means of light.

Operaen by day.   *Operaen at night.*

The Exterior

The external view of the building was very important with its positioning directly on the axis from the Marble Church through the centre of the Royal Palace plaza to the Opera House on the island. The desire to allow the eye to be drawn to the interior was very much in our minds from the beginning. To have the building function as a lantern seemed to talk about the function and experience of being at the opera.

There is no illumination of the stone facing of the building, rather the window slots glow and the large roof floats on a bed of light. The people mingling in the foyer are in dynamic silhouette when viewed from the plaza.

The public plaza on the island in front of the building is lit very simply by three components; minimal stainless steel poles with glowing cylindrical upper sections in two heights utilising dimmable fluorescent lamps; rows of seven LED points randomly located across the plaza (the seven points of light is a recurring theme); linear lighting within handrails to illuminate stairs and the bridges that link to the island. Normally there is no vehicular traffic so when cars are permitted to access the plaza in front of the entrance to drop off and

The Plaza at night.   *The stainless steel lighting poles.*

The glow from the interior and the floating roof.

collect opera-goers the white LED's on the car route itself automatically change to blue, assisting with guiding of vehicles and warning pedestrians.

There was much discussion about the uplighting of the main roof but, with the metal material forming the underside having a high gloss factor, it was agreed that the reflected glare from the roof would have been too disturbing. Instead the glow from the interior was deemed to be adequate.

Main Foyer

Internally the main foyer is dominated by the expressed curved external form of the auditorium volume, referred to by the team as the "conch". This was to be washed with light to bring out the tones and quality of the maple panels and to ensure the eye was drawn to the inside. It was agreed that the curved timber panels would be finished matt to avoid reflections of the lighting equipment but at the last minute the architects changed their mind so the panels are now 'marked' with reflections.

The "conch" is lit from lighting equipment recessed in a slot within the roof light crowning the space. It was felt that whilst the Copenhagen summers are very beautiful and light, the grey winter days generate a quality of light that

The blue sky light above the foyers.   *The cove lighting.*

is not visually positive, so the concept was to use cool colour temperature lamps to provide a fresh impression during the day. Obviously this cool colour appearance would not be conducive to an evening ambience so a second warmer colour temperature is used to wash the timber in the evenings.

At the top of the "conch" the large roof-light allows natural light into the inner part of the foyer and at night these apertures are lit in blue to crown the space and contrast to the orange appearance of the timber panels.

Ground floor view of the foyers.

We were very keen to avoid peppering the ceiling planes with downlights, desiring instead clean surfaces that meant you could look up through the volumes and not be blinded by a battery of downlights. It was therefore decided to illuminate the space by reflected light using the floor zones. A special cove detail was developed with the architects to wrap around the openings in the floor plates. Similar to the lighting of the "conch" the cove has fully dimmable fluorescent sources in two colour temperatures – a cool daylight

The foyer chandeliers.

appearance of 4,000 Kelvin for daytime and a much warmer 2,700 Kelvin for the evenings. The space feels as if it suffused with light rather than being lit. The crossover between these sources is programmed with a very long fade time to avoid the change becoming noticeable if the public are in the foyers during this period. The entire lighting in the foyer changes very slowly and subtly as daylight fails.

The three major dichroic glass chandeliers were designed by the talented Danish/Icelandic artist Olafur Eliasson.

Auditorium

The auditorium provides a major contrast to the white colour palette of the foyer; it has a more intimate and calm feel, almost womb-like. In addition to the problems of achieving an exciting lighting scheme within the auditorium, the acousticians formulated an understandably tough brief with regard to noise from lamp filament hum, from fixtures making noise whilst cooling down and from buzzing transformers. Every single luminaire, lamp and transformer type we wanted to use was thoroughly tested by Arup Acoustics to ensure it met their expectations. Nothing was left to chance.

When you enter the corridors that lead to the auditorium within the 'conch', the lighting is asymmetrically located to wash down the outer wall. The wall was coloured red to create a strong statement in contrast to the previous experience of the white interior within the lobby. Passing through this zone also provides an opportunity to begin to adapt the eye to the lower light levels within the auditorium.

Corridors to the auditorium.

One of the early decisions made prior to our involvement was the use of fibre-optic lighting for the majority of the seating areas. This meant that the noisy illuminators could be located outside of the acoustic auditorium box. We supported this decision and organised a series of mock-ups and tests to ensure we achieved the necessary distribution and illumination intensity. Each of the 2,500 fibre lens heads is carefully focussed and locked in position onto a specific seat or space. This took a considerable time to implement and then check. Apart from the obvious acoustic benefits, the maintenance of the majority of the lighting within the auditorium is therefore incredibly simple and straightforward. The careful focusing of the fibres should never be disturbed as all they require is a gentle dusting. The illuminators are remotely installed in places where they can be accessed when required.

As part of the recurring theme the fibre heads were clustered in linear groups of seven. As the original layout developed groups of five heads appeared practicable but during the consideration of one of the mock-ups the theatre consultant pointed out that the Maersk star has seven points and this change was implemented, providing the benefit of more light sources.

The main area of the stalls is lit by Source 4 profile lanterns deeply recessed within the stage lighting slots within the impressive gold leaf ceiling. During the design process there was considerable discussion as to the nature and design of the ceiling. The gold leaf ceiling was the clients' favoured choice

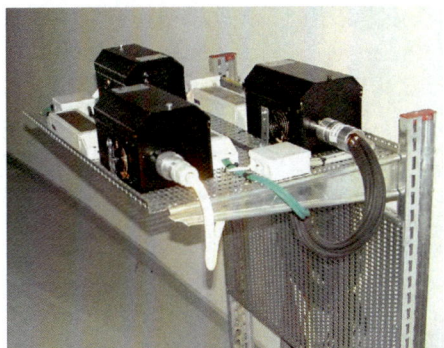
Fibre-optic illuminators.

Fibre optic cables in auditorium soffits.

Auditorium lighting.

The Maersk star.   *Auditorium lighting.*

and we chose to wash across the gold leaf from Source 4 Par lanterns located on the technical gallery. The nature of the gold leaf means that the ceiling changes its appearance dependent upon from where you are viewing it. To contrast with the wash lighting we recessed linear clusters of seven fibre-optic heads to provide sparkle, rather than illumination. All the maintenance of the ceiling lighting is easily achieved from within the technical space inside the roof.

The balcony fronts have a series of linear glowing slots to help break up their mass and to provide the contemporary equivalent of the illuminated glass balcony fixture. These sources are a linear line of long life LEDs behind a specially tinted piece of glass. Again these were tested by the acousticians to ensure they did not compromise their exacting noise requirements. These illuminated slots balance with the acoustic modelling and openings for brackets and connections for lighting and other technical equipment which may need to be used on the balcony fronts.

Within the auditorium all the fibre head groups and LED units are individually addressable by DMX. This allows many permutations fading out the houselights before a performance is about to begin and bringing up the lighting again in an interval. The inspiration behind this was the chandeliers in the Lincoln Centre in New York that are drawn up into the ceiling as the performance is about to begin to enhance the sense of expectation of the audience.

The perimeter timber wall is washed from recessed low voltage sources and where the stepped

The ceiling showing the fibre-optics, the stalls lighting and the special fittings on the technical gallery.

The balcony-front lighting.

The auditorium and stage.

The house curtain with the surtitle screen in view (the screen is normally raised out of view when the house lights are on).

The side walls and first balcony.

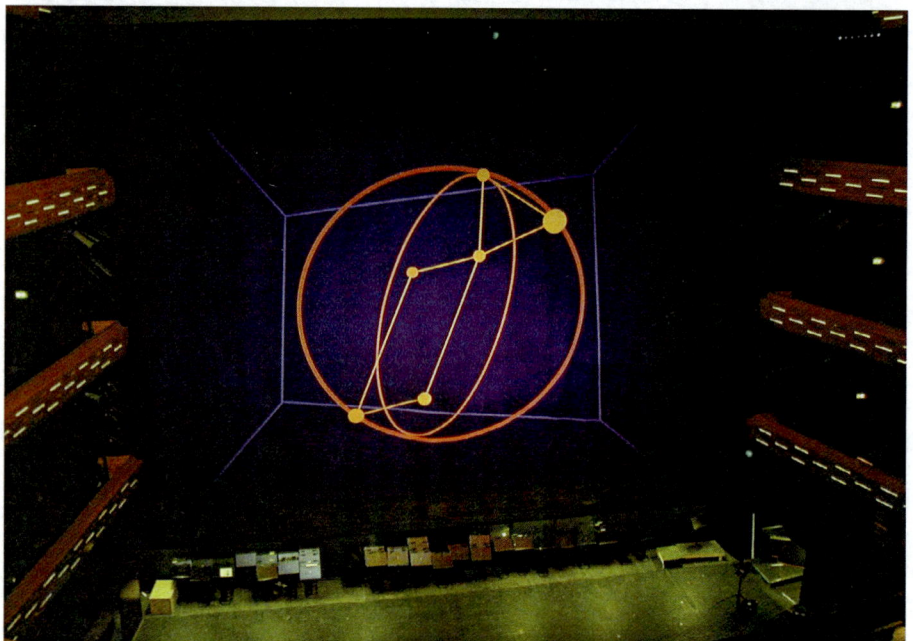
The act cloth designed by Per Arnoldi.

breaks in the walls occur, a linear side-emitting fibre-optic source softly brings this architectural detail into view.

The specially commissioned act cloth was painted by the Danish artist Per Arnoldi and a lot of attention was given to its lighting which was installed in addition to the full stage lighting rig. The design uses strong colours with blue, red and yellow being dominant. Red and blue filtered sources were used to draw out these colours and to also create varying movement from the coloured graphics. This is a very subtle effect but most noticeable by its absence when the lighting is off. The cloth is normally hung downstage of the house curtain so that it can be used to reveal a scene as an alternative to the use of the main red curtain.

Acoustic banners lowered.

Orchestra Rehearsal Room

The orchestra rehearsal room is located five storeys below ground level with an acoustic specification as precise as that for the auditorium. The room is a substantial area approximately 20 metres square by 10 metres high. The brief from the Royal Theatre orchestra for illumination levels was numerically very precise, requiring 850 lux on the working plane, which in this instance was the height of a music stand. Additionally the orchestra were very knowledgeable about the positive colour rendering of tungsten light sources rather than fluorescent or high intensity discharge sources. The orchestra had spent many year rehearsing in their old space which was lit to the same light level but uses industrial type pendant lighting. In the new rehearsal room we had the

The orchestra rehearsal room.

opportunity to provide both functional light and architecturally sensitive light, both to a very high standard.

The luminaires to provide the specific light levels at the working plane were to be provided in the form of a grid of downlight luminaires mounted in the wave like timber ceiling structure. These low-glare luminaires, helped by their mounting in an unconventional ceiling, provided the necessary intensity of light required without creating any distracting glare. Luminaires were tested for their acoustic performance and with the guidance of the acousticians the lighting designers were able to define what dimmed outputs were acceptable within the demanding acoustic brief. Above and beyond the numeric light levels, the room needed to feel positive psychologically given that it is a totally subterranean chamber 17 metres below ground. Vertical illumination in general serves to make a larger space feel comfortable. The timber walls were a perfect surface to take light from dimmable, compact fluorescent 'wall wash' luminaires.

The orchestra rehearsal room ceiling and wall washing 'daylight effect'.

However it was felt that psychologically the orchestra needed some further support and assistance. We discussed an option where we could generate a sense of 'daylight filtering in from a clerestory'. If we could achieve this then we felt that we would be able to make a considerable difference to the ambience of this large subterranean space, especially over the lengths of time the orchestra would be using it. This effect was achieved by working with the architect to allow the wave ceiling to be spaced back from the wall and installing a linear, daylight colour temperature, fluorescent source around the perimeter at high level. We specifically wanted this light to appear to drop off as it travelled down the wall. An even distribution would not have given the same impression of daylight. To further enhance the effect of daylight, the perimeter luminaires are controlled from a daylight sensor mounted on the building roof, which provided information about the actual brightness of the sky. The luminaires increase or decrease in output to mimic the daylight. Therefore the artificial light allows the room to breathe and become animated by light in the same way as a room benefiting from natural light. The orchestra therefore receive both a sense of the lighting conditions externally but also a connection to the outside world. The reaction to the space by the orchestra has been very positive.

The two higher auditorium tiers with the technical level above.

13
SOUND TECHNOLOGY IN OPERAEN Charles Wass, Richard Brett

The complexity of the sound, video and communications infrastructure for a modern opera house may not be quite as extensive as that in a television or radio broadcasting complex or even as that for the Kodak Theatre in Hollywood, but it comes a close second. Not only is there a requirement for high-quality sound and video distribution, extensive communications, and paging systems, there are also the special facilities for the reproduction and balancing of the electronic sound within the auditorium, cueing systems, show relay and opera surtitles.

Theatreplan were commissioned to direct and control these parts of the technical installations. Theatreplan's Charles Wass, who had previously prepared the designs for the sound and communications infrastructure of the Gran Teatre del Liceu in Barcelona, had worked previously with Eric Pressley on the Royal Opera House installations and he and Eric were joined by Rick Clarke to form a planning group. This combined extensive theatre consulting experience and current opera house practice with Rick's knowledge of loudspeakers and sound design gained from his work in the West End and on tour internationally. In this way all the critical aspects of the sound and communications system design had the right level of expertise and there was sufficient overlap of knowledge and opinion to allow meaningful debate and discussion. Charles was project leader, while Eric planned the majority of the infrastructure and Rick developed a sound system to provide a very high quality of sound in the three-tier auditorium.

Although the preliminary planning of the systems was done before Theatreplan were allowed to talk to the Royal Theatre, when the proposed infrastructure schemes were put to the Royal's sound team they were largely accepted. The details were discussed at length and the principles agreed. There were however some interesting changes which the Royal wanted: one of these was the introduction of a large number of 100v line circuits for feeding loudspeakers, both around the stage and auditorium as well as in remote locations, such as rehearsal rooms. The Royal had been using a number of 100v line loudspeakers in the scenery and settings and in their second auditorium at Kongens Nytorv and seemed wedded to using these. In fact they were not very keen on having low-impedance wiring at all and, although such wiring was deleted from the tender documents, it was later reinstated after the contract was signed.

The infrastructure is extensive, covering the sound, communications, video and control systems within the auditorium and stage, the paging to the foyers and the paging and show relay backstage, cueing and stage management systems and the surtitle installations. The foyers, production offices and rehearsal rooms all have audio and video tie-lines which allow the distribution of signals between most of the areas in which any sort of presentation, rehearsal, social or technical activity was considered likely to take place. The physical method of installing this was on cable tray throughout the building as we were advised that trunking and conduit could not be used in Denmark. The distribution of video uses a single cable for both analogue and digital signals, but the available equivalent cable for audio was insufficiently robust to be laid on tray and so two cables had to be installed, one for analogue and one for digital audio. Later we learned that trunking and conduit were installed to provide protection and ferrous shielding in radio and television studios in Denmark and so a more robust installation would have been possible. The project electrical contractor, Kemp and Lauritzen, who installed the cable tray did agree to use protective pipes for the sound system cables in critical areas such as in the side and rear stages. Their contract included all the tray for the sound, communications, video and control wiring, onto which the sound and video systems contractor, Informationstechnik AS, laid the wiring. Kemp and Lauritzen played a large part in the installation of the theatre technical equipment as they provided all the power distribution for the stage and work lighting and the power supplies for all the extensive stage engineering installations.

This wiring infrastructure, including fibre-optic lines from the sound control room, mixing positions in the auditorium, the rehearsal rooms, recording studio and from the studio stage, terminates largely in the Sound Equipment Rack Room in the first level understage on stage right (when looking at the auditorium, or Konge side in Danish). Every effort was made in the early planning of the building to find a location near the 'centre of gravity' of the wiring infrastructure. A reasonable area was identified but, as every experienced consultant knows, cables routes are not always what they appear, and for many months headroom limits and other restrictions caused headaches while trying to get the multitudes of cables across stage without having to go right around the mainstage elevator pit. Adjacent to the sound equipment rack room is a small sound studio with a control room and a sound equipment store. A goods lift serves the stage and other levels and a more accessible store also exists at stage level.

The sound system in the auditorium was planned by Rick and debated at length with Charles and Eric before being agreed. Based on Rick's positive experience of distributed arrays it was proposed to install a number of discrete loudspeakers in the header of the architectural proscenium, together with four loudspeakers stacked above each other on each side, each approximately at

Downstage left showing loudspeakers in the architectural proscenium.

the level of the audience in the stalls and on each tier. The upper tier is in fact a technical walkway which is at the level of the acoustic reflector and carries both stage and house lighting fittings. Rick proposed d&b loudspeakers because their performance matched what he knew the auditorium would require. Visits to various London theatres, including West End shows, were therefore arranged for the Head of Sound of the Royal Theatre to review and evaluate a number of systems.

There is a complication in the Copenhagen opera introduced by the theatre planners! The architectural proscenium is moveable: not up and down stage, but the header can be raised and lowered and the two side towers can both be moved on and off-stage to a limited degree. This is so that the proscenium opening as defined by the opera portal (or false proscenium) upstage does not appear out of proportion to the room: the scale of the stage end of the room can be adjusted by the architectural proscenium to relate to the proscenium opening. It also allows a very wide and high stage to be created. This staging facility does set the sound designers a problem. However, after considering the degree of movement entailed it was established that the change to the sound field coverage would be small and acceptable.

While initially liking the proposed scheme, the head of sound at the Royal Theatre became uneasy and requested the use of different loudspeakers, ones which he knew and had used before. While this made Rick less happy, all sound and lighting designers do have personal preferences and most systems can be adapted to use loudspeakers from an alternative range. Thus a system based around L'Acoustics loudspeakers was developed, but the Theatreplan team were rather nonplussed when a horizontal line array was requested as a central cluster rather than the distributed loudspeakers in the architectural proscenium. Much of the collaboration with the acoustics consultants, Arup Acoustics, had been based on the design team understanding that extremely good natural room acoustics were a high priority in this project. Much effort had been put into hiding the loudspeakers in the architectural proscenium so that there could be no visual implication that the orchestra or singers were ever being 'miked' and the sound reinforced. To have a separately-hoisted central cluster dropped into view was considered unfortunate for opera. In fact a loudspeaker hoist had been provided but this was intended for the occasional musical or similar presentation when the opera were on holiday in the summer break. Rick had used line arrays on tour where rigging time was short but neither he or Eric felt that such an array was ideal to provide the coverage of a three-tier opera house where good coverage and a high sound pressure level was required. One of the principles on which Theatreplan operates when working with an experienced, professional client is to go through all the reasoning, demonstrations and discussions and after this, if the user has a specific requirement which is not completely unacceptable, to make every effort to accommodate that requirement. While not being happy with this approach, this is what happened in this instance. The hidden openings in the top of the architectural proscenium remain for use in the future.

In addition to the proscenium arrays, both under-balcony delay speakers and surround sound units are installed. The delays are to ensure those in the rear of each tier, who get good natural sound but for whom the main cluster is out of sight, can hear any reinforced sound. The surround-sound loudspeakers are largely for effects which are becoming more part of modern opera production. A pair of large bass-bins which were far too large to fit in the architectural proscenium are, despite the concerns of the architects, mounted on the acoustic reflector. All these loudspeakers and those in the proscenium zone are fed from an amplifier room on the Konge side of the auditorium at technical gallery level so as to minimise cable runs. Both the delay and surround loudspeakers had their problems as, because of the need

Construction of third tier showing timber formers for loudspeakers.

to minimise the depth of the balcony structure, the layout of the units had to be designed before the auditorium finishes and openings were cast into the concrete infill. When the architects came to detail the soffits and to co-ordinate the loudspeakers, fibre-optic lighting and other services with the finishes, some things were not positioned correctly and some loudspeaker units had to be omitted. In addition, the carefully designed and prototyped loudspeaker covers which had a large number of specifically-sized holes to give 53% open area, as considered acceptable both by Theatreplan and the architects, were never actually delivered. The manufacturer apparently supplied panels with smaller holes and a spacing offering only 38% open area. Despite this and although some of the loudspeakers that were fitted are not in optimum positions, the coverage is remarkably good and shows the importance of designing to achieve more than is required. The contractor always has a way out when finishes are being fitted late in a contract as he only has to say that it is not possible to produce new panels in time and the incorrect items have to be accepted! Theatreplan were not directly involved in such negotiations on this issue but

Auditorium showing orchestra pit markings and production desks.

it is galling when a prototype has been made correctly and the quantity items supplied by the same manufacturer differ significantly.

To complete the auditorium installation a number of image shift loudspeakers are installed in the stage front edge. This was a particularly heavily serviced zone with a very pleasing structural solution based on a design proposal by Theatreplan which minimised the thickness of the orchestra pit overhang. While the overhang does not normally form part of the orchestra pit as the Royal Theatre musicians prefer not to play under any cover, it can provide additional acoustic volume in the pit. It also accommodates the prompt box elevator. Small loudspeakers which could provide the right sound pressure level and distribution were required and here Eric was able to turn the tables on the Royal by suggesting that a very good unit for this application would be one from L'Acoustics! These sit in restricted depth of the floor along with video cameras for the conductor, traps for floats (footlights), production lighting outlets, sound and communications panels and a lot of wiring.

The front end of the sound system also went through a number of changes. The Royal Theatre were using Yamaha PM1D digital consoles in their existing theatres and the original plan was that these would also be specified for the new opera. In this way all the staff would all be competent to operate sound in any of the venues. Where such arrangements can be made, this is a practical solution. The PM1D has 48 A&B inputs giving it a 96 input capability. Although not designed for live sound mixing in a theatre it is a practical piece of equipment, although very large to move into the stalls or dress circle for sound balancing in the auditorium. The sound control room, along with that for lighting and a central scenic projection position, is at the rear of the first tier. The sound control room is fitted with a sliding glass single-glazed window which is hauled up and down by a small hoist unit and which is compressed between pneumatic seals in its raised position. Moving the Yamaha out of the control room might require a team of strong people to get it out though the open window and then through the foyers and down stairs to the stalls entrance. Not really an appropriate approach in a major opera house.

Accordingly two control surfaces were specified for use at the two levels. All major projects understandably attract the interest of equipment suppliers and so along comes the local dealer for Studer, offering a special deal on a far more compact Studer Vista 8 digital desk. The Royal were enthusiastic about this desk. Problem solved, although the Studer is also not designed primarily for live venue sound mixing and has very noisy processing racks

Three control room windows at rear of first balcony.

that in a recording studio would go in the equipment room. As noisy racks could not be accommodated in the theatre sound control room they had always been planned to be in the sound equipment rack room where they only annoy other signal processing equipment! Fibre-optic cables link the processors to the various positions in which the mixing console can be used: sound control room, front of the first tier and in the stalls, clear of the overhang.

Although the Studer was a more economic purchase, what was overlooked was the loss of the A&B facility. It was a 48 channel desk. However by this time Studer were beginning to realise the application of this console in performance venues and came up with a new configuration giving all the master

Mixing consoles in sound control room.

controls and one set of channel controls in one pod and two more sets of channel controls in a second pod, both pods being good ergonomically and able to be picked up and relocated without needing a removal crew. All the processing is now remote so the units are easier to handle. This is a good solution and allows the two controls to be used in any combination wherever they are required.

The other sound system peripherals for use around the building are all mounted in a set of wheeled mobile racks which can be connected with multi-pin connectors in the control rooms, the recording studio, rehearsal rooms, in the studio stage and similar. There are some 26 units of a number of different configurations offering sound and video facilities for replay, recording, editing, effects and also rehearsal use by non-technical staff. This approach is very flexible and makes for easy movement of the required facility and easy control. The Royal Theatre did not want any specific repititeurs' facilities for use backstage as these were not something they had used before. However the lighting people, who deal with cueing and intercoms for the Royal, did wish to implement the cueing system which they had in the old theatre. This is based on red and green two-digit numbers and an additional set of coloured lights. It does not incorporate the 'acknowledge standby' facility of a return signal to the stage manager which has become standard in many countries. Although you need to be given the knowledge to interpret these numbers and lights it is clearly a very comprehensive system allowing complex instructions to be given to those in the know. You also need to have the calling system from the rehearsal rooms explained to you in case, as a visiting artiste, you hear a short piece of music from *Tannhäuser* or *the Marriage of Figaro* over the PA system. It could be your call! Voice paging is however provided to the dressing rooms, offices and foyers from the main stage and studio stage, together with show relay sound.

The stage management, cueing, intercom, paging and show relay systems were planned by Charles

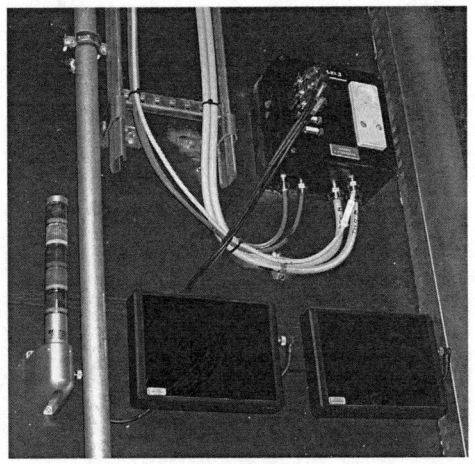

The Royal Theatre's cueing system.

Wass and Eric Pressley and included a comprehensive system to distribute sound and calls between the main stage, rehearsal stage, the studio stage, chorus room, orchestra rehearsal hall and all the rehearsal rooms. Calls to the main stage cannot be made during rehearsals or performances and each of the rehearsal spaces had local controls to disable show relay signals. The completed stage management desk and facilities as supplied by Informationstechnik were very satisfactory and in addition had some welcome additional features. The paging was replaced with the musical calls as part of a system negotiated by the Royal Theatre with a local supplier representing Bosch Security Systems. In this installation the paging and show relay are combined with the emergency evacuation announcement system except in the dressing room zones where the system is not automatically monitored but is manually checked monthly. Other communications systems include digital talkback installed throughout the stage and technical areas which interfaces to two rings and to three channels of radio for stage use. There are also radio channels for security and for the fire brigade. This radio coverage and facilities for mobile phones (for crew and performers use!) are extended throughout the building.

Communications desk enclosure.

After the change to 100v line, the wiring on-stage for the fold-back loudspeakers was altered back to low-impedance and the Royal Theatre prepared a list of equipment which they felt they wanted based on their experience on the old stage. This included three types and sizes of loudspeakers including L'Acoustics 115XT loudspeakers and amplifiers. Rather than use these large units on stage they initially tried a number of very small units to provide a reverberant sound field on stage using Genelec 1029A loudspeakers. A consequence of this was that guest artist Roberto Alagna, playing Radames in the dress rehearsal of the opening production, *Aida,* found it impossible to hear himself on stage. Because of the room acoustics implications of this difficulty, Rob Harris of Arup Acoustics reviewed what they were trying to achieve and worked with the Royal sound department, a local sound consultant and the singers to adjust the system. Based on the level of fold-back employed in other opera houses it was felt that Roberto Alagna was probably used to higher levels than were being offered. The Royal Theatre's singers had been used to considerable comfort from the artificial reverberation system installed in their Old Stage. To improve the direct sound any unnecessary drapes were

Stage manager's desk in downstage corner.

removed from the fly tower and the fold-back level increased using simulated reverberance and delays to give additional reflections at +25 ms and +60 ms relative to the direct sound, thus increasing the apparent support to the singers. After the system was set up satisfactorily some of the Royal Theatre singers said that they felt that the fold-back level was actually now too high and that they all needed to learn to sing in the new house! It was hoped that as the singers gain confidence in the house, in the way the orchestra very quickly did, the sound department will be able to slowly reduce the level of support offered. One of the side effects of these investigations was to note the excessive noise on stage during the rehearsals caused by cooling fans for filters on the high powered lights on the upstage cyclorama bar. The measured level within the upstage performing area was 40dB(A) which was 15dB(A) higher than desirable, that is at least twice as noisy as acceptable. This noise was affecting the support available to the singers upstage by masking the fold-back sound. What was more serious was that this noise was clearly audible within the auditorium and indicates the pollution caused by theatre lighting equipment. Arrangements were made to use the remote switching facilities provided as part of the stage lighting infrastructure so that these fans only ran when necessary.

One of the peripheral installations, although important in an opera house,

Auditorium with surtitle screen in position.

was the surtitle system. As described earlier most of the audience do have sight of the main surtitle screen which is suspended downstage of the architectural proscenium and hangs above the portal opening. As it is downstage of the house curtain, the surtitle screen hoist is controlled as part of the power flying system and can be cued to drop silently into position as the house lights dim at the start of the performance and to retract out of sight when they again illuminate the house. Although originally conceived as a video projection system using computer generated images in order to achieve more extensive fonts and increased display capability, projection systems do require setting up whenever the height of the screen is altered and this can be a frequent occurrence in a repertoire opera house. The Royal were hosting a demonstration of an LED display surtitle system by a Danish company, Visutech, to which Theatreplan were invited. Later investigations indicated that this system could offer most of the facilities that were thought to be important and the Visutech were very keen to develop their system to comply with all Theatreplan's particular requirements. They produced the size of main display screen that was required and also developed a small seat back repeater screen for those seats from which one could not see the main display. The main display screen power supplies dissipate significant heat and although the cooling fans turned out to be more noisy than the acousticians could accept, this was resolved by Visutech to everyone's satisfaction. The Visutech system is operated from a computer in one of the production viewing rooms at the rear of the stalls and has proved very satisfactory.

The video installation is extensive and serves every operational and technical area. The infrastructure is designed for 625 line PAL broadcast quality so that the Royal can make recordings for commercial use in the same way as many other opera houses. The video system allows for large number of monitoring cameras for production use and these images appear on the stage manager's and cue master's desks as well as

Equipment within the main Visutech surtitle screen.

being available throughout backstage. The display of the conductor's image caused a problem for the dancers, rather more than the singers, in that the delay caused in the digital flat-screen monitors mounted in the auditorium and around the portal was sufficient to cause them difficulties, even when they couldn't also see the conductor. Tests done at the Royal Opera House in London with a monitor alongside the conductor had much earlier shown the extent of the problem with flat-screen monitors, and that the effect was less with plasma screens rather than with LCD monitors. The problem has been reduced with a change of the type of monitor. The large camera and remote pan and tilt mounting purchased for use in the centre of the first tier balcony front was felt to be unacceptable for the opening and was not fitted until after handover because of its large size! So at least the early publicity photographs are not an advertisement for video equipment!

After some months of operations and after the understandable initial difficulties, the Head of Sound at the Royal, Claus Wolter, was asked his feelings about the sound system and the installations. Naturally he started with some comments about the sound control room, where so much critical work has to be performed. Claus had worked hard to get as large an opening into the auditorium as possible and also wanted to achieve the same ceiling

Lighting equipment and monitor on side balcony.

Flat screen monitor and loudspeaker on architectural proscenium.

line between control room and balcony soffit for acoustic reasons. He is concerned that the sound stops where the window begins so if you want the real auditorium sound, it is necessary to go to the side of the desk and to lean out of the window. He made the point that there is a considerable difference in what you hear when you do this. While this ceiling alignment wasn't achievable, we did manage to get a good-size of window opening (1500 mm high and 3650 mm wide) and large pane of thick glass (12 mm laminated) which lowers mechanically below the sill. When closed, peripheral air seals ensure that there is good sound insulation. This operates very quietly and the construction is arranged so that with the window open the mixing desk can be pushed forward by some 60 cms (2 feet) to the back of the rear row of seats which gives a much better working position. After the change to the Studer Vista 8, Claus reported that these are working perfectly and the sound engineers are getting more and more pleased working with them. His comment was that these are tools you have to study a lot, before you master them!

One thing which both the Royal and Theatreplan wanted was the wiring solution in which all the wiring from all positions in the house, audio, video, analogue and digital terminated in one main patch area. Claus is very proud of this and believes that having a location where all these circuits can be accessed and patched to any place in the house is really a success. There is also a multi-core wiring system which can be patched in the multi-core patch bay and then distributed locally in various locations using splitter boxes. He reports that this is also performing satisfactorily for any show situation and also for broadcasting.

Claus feels that the PA sound system is working well, but he would not recommend to anyone having the main left and right side loudspeakers in a moving wall. He commented that he worked very hard to avoid this, but that he lost. As mentioned above, this was a known difficulty and with this form of proscenium it is very difficult to hide the loudspeakers anywhere, which is what was required. Claus makes the point that if the architectural proscenium, in which the speakers are mounted, are in the smallest position (13m opening), where the speakers are clear of the balcony, everything is fine. But as the proscenium is widened from this position, the sound coverage gets worse. With that qualification he does however report that the delay and surround loudspeakers do what is required of them. After a number of trials the Royal ended up placing the two large subwoofers on top of each other on the acoustic reflector, over the proscenium in the centre of the auditorium, in order to equalise some phasing problems.

The centre cluster which the Royal want to use started life at the wrong tilt angle as there is not enough space in the ceiling above to have it going up at the right angle. Space in the proscenium zone of theatres is always at a premium and the hoist and loudspeaker storage zone did not allow for the size of array now installed. The Royal are determined to find a solution and sadly this is going to require loudspeakers in view for some operas. Claus is looking at an automatic motor system, with which they can preset different heights for different purposes and have the system set to the required tilt angle when the speakers come down through the ceiling. However the ARC's cluster is reported as perfect, and because of the very good acoustics in the auditorium, it gives a very even coverage of all seats; they only miss the two front rows in the stalls a bit, due again to the wrong tilt angle. In addition Claus reports that they are quite happy with the L'Acoustics loudspeaker system and the Sound Web controllers.

Following the initial difficulties with the fold-back, Claus gave his description of what the Royal have developed as a reverb system on the mainstage to help the singers get a feeling of what they are singing. They have placed 10 small 1029 Genelec loudspeakers around the portal opening, facing the stage. On the Lighting Bridge above the portal they have placed two Axys line array

An early rehearsal to check acoustics.

speakers to cover further back on the stage. They then use two AudioTechnica microphones in the technical proscenium and two Crown PZM microphones on the stage floor when necessary. This whole system is controlled by a Yamaha DME64, which they can control remotely by wireless from a Teqsas Reco and this gives the operator the opportunity to hear on the spot, what he or she is providing to the singers.

Despite having been commissioned, the acoustic banners and curtains described as part of the room acoustic adjustments were not working when Claus summarised his feelings on the installations but he did want them back in service as soon as possible. He felt that they would really be a good thing to use, particularly when the Royal are working with electronic amplified productions.

In summary he was kind enough to say that, in his opinion, the Operaen is a very nice and in some ways, perfect, house to work in and it is getting better and better with time.

14 THE ORGAN

The Opera House organ was built by the Allen Organ Company, USA, and it represents the state-of-the-art in this field. It is probably the largest digital organ in Europe. It has 128 speaking stops, four manuals and pedal, and its vast specification allows the organist to perform music from virtually any period in history, from pre-baroque to contemporary.

The console is placed on a mobile dolly and there are five different connection points where it can be positioned for performance. For example, it can be placed centre stage for solo concerts or in the pit with the orchestra or at the back of the stage. An identical array of 28 speakers is installed on either side directly behind the proscenium arch. Hanging on steel beems, they face the concrete wall, reflecting the sound so that it projects out into the auditorium. Half of the speakers are JBL high efficiency speakers and the other half are normal Allen Herald cabinets. The system has 24 channels, including eight huge bass cabinets in order to produce a bass that can match a full orchestra.

The total power is 2800 Watts RMS producing sounds from 16 Hz to 20.000 Hz.

Per Frendahl, the Allen Organ Company representative for Sweden and Denmark, was responsible for the specification and installation of the instrument in conjunction with Søren Nylin, technical consultant, The Royal Danish Theatre.

Copenhagen Opera House 221

Pedal
32 Principal Basse
32 Contre Bourdon
32 Contre Violone
16 Contre Basse
16 Bourdon
16 Bourdon doux (Sw)
16 Violone
16 Quintaten (Ch)
16 Erzähler (Ch)
10 2/3 Gross Quinte
8 Octave Basse
8 Spitz Geigen
8 Flûte à Cheminée
8 Cor de Nuit (Sw)
8 Gambe (Gt)
5 1/3 Quinte
4 Octave
4 Choralbass
4 Flûte
2 Flûte
Fourniture IV
Cymbale III
32 Contre Bombarde
32 Contre Basson
16 Bombarde
16 Basson
16 Trompette (Sw)
8 Trompeta Real (So)
8 Trompette
8 Basson
4 Basson
4 Clairon
4 Chalumeau (Ch)
Tremulant
Chimes
8 Great To Pedal
8 Swell To Pedal
4 Swell To Pedal
8 Choir To Pedal
8 Solo To Pedal
MIDI On Pedal

Choir
16 Quintaten
16 Erzähler
16 Erzähler Celeste
8 Montre
8 Bourdon
8 Quintadena
8 Voce Umana
8 Erzähler
8 Erzähler Celeste
4 Prestant
4 Flûte à Fuseau
4 Lieblichflöte
4 Erzähler
4 Erzähler Celeste
2 2/3 Nazard
2 Doublette
2 Quarte de Nazard
1 3/5 Tierce
1 1/3 Larigot
1 Sifflöte
Cornet VI (So)
Cymbale III
Fourniture III
16 Doucaine
8 Trompeta Real (So)
8 Trompette
8 Cromorne
4 Chalumeau
Tremulant
Tremulant Full
Chimes
Celesta
Orchestral Harp
Handbells
Harpsichord
Zimbelstern

Unison Off
16 Swell To Choir
8 Swell To Choir
4 Swell To Choir
8 Solo To Choir
MIDI On Choir

Swell

16 Bourdon doux
8 Principal
8 Flûte Bouchée
8 Cor de Nuit
8 Flûte Dolce
8 Flûte Céleste
8 Viole de Gambe
8 Voix Céleste
4 Octave
4 Flûte Octaviante
2 2/3 Nazard
2 Octavin
2 Flûte à Bec
1 3/5 Tierce
1 Sifflet
Plein Jeu IV
16 Contre Trompette
16 Basson
8 Trompette Harmonique
8 Hautbois
8 Voix Humaine
4 Clairon Harmonique
4 Hautbois-Clairon
Tremulant
Tremulant Full
16 Swell To Swell
Unison Off
4 Swell To Swell

The organ on its mobile 'dolly', pictured sidestage.

8 Solo To Swell
MIDI On Swell

Solo
8 Diapason
8 Flauto Mirabilis
4 Octave
4 Flauto Traverso2 Super Octave
Cornet VI
16 Trompeta Real
16 Bombarde
8 Trompeta Real
8 Trompette
8 French Horn
8 Corno di Bassetto
8 English Horn
4 Trompeta Real
4 Clairon
Tremulant
MIDI On Solo

Great
32 Bourdon
16 Bourdon
16 Violone
8 Montre
8 Flûte Harmonique
8 Flûte à Cheminée
8 Gambe
5 1/3 Gross Nazard
4 Prestant
Flûte
3 1/5 Gross Tierce
2 2/3 Quinte
2 Doublette
2 Waldflöte
Fourniture V
Cornet V
Grande Fourniture II-IV
Cymbale IV
16 Bombarde
8 Trompeta Real (So)
8 Trompette
4 Clairon
Tremulant
Tremulant Full
Chimes
Unison Off
16 Swell To Great
8 Swell To Great
4 Swell To Great
8 Choir To Great
8 Solo To Great
MIDI On Great

Generals
All Swells To Swell
Solo Unenclosed
Gt-Pd Unenclosed
Choir Unenclosed
Manual

The stage right organ speaker assembly.

16 Off
Mixtures Off
Reeds Off
Melody Coupler So>Gt
Bass Coupler
Gt-Ch Manual Transfer
Alternate Tuning
Solo Mains Off

Solo Antiphonal On
Swell Mains Off
Swell Antiphonal On
Gt-Pd Mains Off
Gt-Pd Antiphonal On
Choir Mains Off
Choir Antiphonal On

Virtuoso organist Carlo Curley checks out the Opera House organ.

15 THE VIEWS OF THE USERS

These responses were sought after the Royal Theatre had been in the new Opera House for just over half their first season.

Technical Director, Nikolaj Jensen

In the year 2000 we received the message that the Royal Theatre had been given a gift in the shape of a new opera house – a gift you don't receive every day.

Many thoughts and ideas went through our heads as we were to take part in creating as optimal a house as possible. We had to work fast to live up to the tight schedule. We had to take thousands of decisions in no time which all had to be right. But we had very good assistance from the advisers on stage technology.

From the start we had some basic principles which we aimed to keep to during the whole process:
- We had to have as good logistics as possible.
- We had to have an optimal and safe working environment.
- We had to have the best technical solutions and installations.
- We had to have maximum flexibility.
- We had to have freedom to create daylight in every room where it was possible.

These basic principles have, by and large, been fulfilled to our great satisfaction. There have been a countless number of decisions during the building activities which had to be made and vast number of solutions had to be found. So it has altogether been a great and extensive decision-making process.

All this would not have been possible if we had not also had among our staff, some members who had accumulated over several years expert knowledge in connection with the building and renovation of theatres.

One requirement is knowledge concerning technical possibilities and solutions. Another large and complicated need is organisation; the handling of staff and recruitment of additional personnel. So in 2002, the Royal Theatre started an evaluation process and introduced the procedure of assigning tasks throughout the team and establishing far greater empowerment within the management structure than had been seen previously.

This was based on the five shared values of The Royal Theatre which are:
- Respect
- Professional pride
- Empathy
- Dialogue
- Committed community

These were decided upon and laid down by all our employees, and were discussed, understood and are now complied with by all! At the same time approximately 100 managers had supplementary training in different personal and management values and abilities. This was to ensure that delegation and the resulting empowerment were clearly understood, and that the managers had enough 'tools' and a secure basis on which to carry this out. In addition a number of courses providing factual knowledge about machinery, operations, safety and so on were held. The recruiting and introduction of nearly a further 100 new staff members was also carefully arranged and undertaken, so that the best staff members with the right professional and personal qualities were engaged.

To make sure that everybody followed the planned schedule and to ensure that the correct information was available we started a plan of action approximately two years before moving in to the new house. This plan contained a point for every area where action had to be taken before we could move in. The plan was revised every second week and presented to a group formed of Heads of Departments which considered the available information and decided on the necessary actions and followed this through as necessary. At the same time we put together a budget for each area where we were fitting out the building; for example for IT, where the Head of the IT Department could decide his priorities within his field. In this way we ensured a non-bureaucratic situation in which decisions were made on the level of the expert knowledge.

The initiative described above secured that, by and large, everybody had their hearts in the right place and achieved a miraculous effort which meant that we were able to move in during the three and a half months from when we took possession of the house on 1 October 2004 until we opened on 15 January 2005. This miraculous effort has continued since. We only had one technical accident in the whole first half of the first season which set us back 11 minutes during *Aida*, otherwise all performances were carried through as planned.

The Opera at work.

Opera Director, Kasper Holten

It has been a great experience to start using the new opera house in Copenhagen. The house has been planned and built to give ideal conditions for artistic development and, even if there has been a lot to get used to for us, as well as opening problems which had to be managed, one has to say that with the gift of the opera house we have received a fantastic building which gives us the possibility to perform opera on a modern level.

The most important features are naturally, first and foremost, that we have got so much extra space and also that on the stage we have got so many new technical possibilities to play with. It will be really exciting as the use of the house develops, when, as an artist begins to play with new narrative styles, new technical possibilities open up. The technical facilities are, in themselves, an empty display but they give us the possibility to work with some new dramaturgic possibilities and then they become really interesting.

In *Siegfried* I had the chance to use the technical facilities to enhance the production. As more of the family secrets hidden in the basement are revealed, so the stage engineering enables us to lift the set from the dark repression of the basement into the daylight. The repression and the process whereby the truth is coming into the light are illustrated by the movement of the setting and do not have to be explained further. Later in *Siegfried* the principal character is approaching a distant mountain and here we had the possibility to have the mountain glide slowly downstage, while revolving, from the furthest rear stage, with a colossal effective scenic depth as the result.

But daily I notice perhaps most of all the light everywhere in the house. We theatre people are used to working in dark rooms and walking in out-of-the-way corridors without windows. You can't leave a rehearsal room in the new opera house without meeting a fantastic view over the port of Copenhagen from where the light pours in, so you live with the changes of the seasons and the course of the day. It means a tremendously improved working environment, and all foreign artists who come to visit us are dizzy with envy and very impressed by the new house and all its possibilities.

Ballet Director, Frank Andersen

As the opening gala event was taking place on 15 January 2005, it was obvious that the Opera would open a new and exciting chapter in the story of The Royal Theatre. Now we would have the artistic and physical opportunities provided by three professional stages – three stages, two houses, and infinite possibilities. Possibilities we have been looking forward to seize and by which to be challenged.

We had already taken advantage of the wonderful facilities provided by the small stage of the Opera, Takkelloftet, for our childrens' and school performances where the youngest can now experience dance in an intimate forum. The stage has already proved its worth for neo-classic ballet and modern dance and it also provides us with the capacity for experimental projects and will make an extra contribution for the expansion and development of the company's choreographic talents.

Big stages come with great ambitions – and great expectations. The company's first performance on the main stage of the Opera had to be nothing less than a new masterpiece, which used and combined all the latent potential in choreography, design, drama and music. Choreographer John Neumeier and the company defied initial technical and logistic difficulties and conquered the Opera with *The Little Mermaid* which fulfilled all the expectations of both audience and critics.

The Royal Ballet will always have its headquarters on Gamle Scene, Kongens Nytorv, where the history of Denmark's national company originates. Here Bournonville founded his special aesthetic and beloved ballets; here the ballet school has nurtured talents and launched star dancers over some 200 years. The building itself exudes great experiences and historic events and now the new Opera has to make its own history. The Royal Ballet is looking forward to writing the first chapters.

16 TECHNICAL SCHEDULES

Stage Engineering Installations
General parameters

OVERSTAGE POWER FLYING	
Height of grid above stage	30 metres
Number of across stage bars	87
Length of bars	22 metres
Number of suspension wire ropes	7
Number of up-down stage bars	3
Flying bars centres	200 mm (8")
Maximum load and speed	800 kg at up to 900 mm/second
Maximum speed and load	400 kg at up to 1800 mm/second
Number of point hoists	24 (4 in each bay)
Maximum load and speed	500 kg at up to 900 mm/second
Maximum speed and load	250 kg at up to 1800 mm/second
All flying equipment operated by stage control system	

STAGE CONTROL SYSTEM	
Operational Control Panels	8 CAT 180, each with 5 and 10 metre leads
Riggers Control Panels	3 CAT 100, each with 5 and 10 metre leads
Secondary Control Panels	2 CAT 60 each with 5 and 10 metre leads
Remote Radio Pendant	1 CAT 100R
Simultaneous operations	16 control panels can be connected to the system and used simultaneously
Stage control system operates overstage flying (bars and point hoists), lighting windlasses, and mainstage elevators	

LIGHTING WINDLASSES	
Number of windlasses	5 each side of stage plus 2 up-stage for back light bar

Copenhagen Opera House 233

Cables on each windlass	3
Power supply capacity in each cable	60 amps 3-phase, neutral and earth
Control circuits in each cable	3 x CAT5
Number of windlasses normally feeding one set of across-stage lighting frames	2, one from each side
Length of each lighting frame	3 metres
Number of bars normally carrying lighting frames	4, giving a load capacity of 3,200 kg

ROLLING CYCLORAMA

Length of header	52 metres
Overall height in use	23.5 metres
Distance raised to store	4.5 metres
Time to raise or lower	Approximately 35 secs
Time to extend or retract	Approximately 4 minutes

ARCHITECTURAL PROSCENIUM

Maximum opening	17.25m wide x 13m high
Minimum opening	13m wide by 11m high

OPERA PORTAL	
Maximum opening	16 metres wide x 11 metres high
Minimum opening	12 metres wide x 7.5 metres high
Maximum height of opening	12.5 metres high (special adjustment)
Distributed payload on lighting bridge	7,000 kg
Distributed payload on each tormentor tower	1,500 kg
MAINSTAGE ELEVATORS	
Number of mainstage elevators	4
Plan area of each elevator	16 x 4 metres
Maximum static load	48,000 kg
Maximum dynamic load	32,000 kg
Maximum load and speed	32,000 kg at up to 120 mm/second
Maximum speed and load	16,000 kg at up to 250 mm/second
Maximum travel	From 5 metres below stage to 5 metres above
Travel of lower platform	From 5 metres below stage to 2.5 metres below
Mainstage elevators operated by stage control system or by local engineering control	
CLOTH STORAGE ELEVATOR	
Plan size of elevator	23 metres x 2 metres wide (upstage)
Length of cloth storage racks	23 metres
Number of racks	8 on each side
Maximum load capacity of each rack	1,200 kg
Speed of raise and lower	150 mm/second
Maximum height above stage	7.75 metres
Cloth storage elevator operated by its own local hand-held controllers, one at each end	

Copenhagen Opera House 235

STAGE WAGONS	
Height of all stage wagons	300 mm
Number of full-size stage wagons	10
Plan size of full-size stage wagon	16 x 4 metres
Distributed dynamic load on full-size wagon	16,000 kg
Number of half-size stage wagons	5 (one fills in the downstage area through the portal)
Plan size of half-size stage wagon	16 x 2 metres
Distributed dynamic load on half-size wagon	8,000 kg
Maximum point load on any stage wagon	Local loads up to 7.5 kN/m^2 or 3,000 kg on a 200 x 200mm area
Maximum speed of motion	300 mm/sec (18 metres/minute)
Stage wagons operated by the stage wagon controls in the vicinity of each move	
BALLET WAGON	
Plan size of ballet wagon	16 x 16 metres
Distributed dynamic load	20,000 kg
Distributed static load	40,000 kg
Local loading on ballet wagon floor	2.5 kN/m^2
Maximum speed of motion	300 mm/sec (18 metres/minute)
Stage wagons operated by the stage wagon controls in the vicinity of each move	

REVOLVE WAGON	
Plan size of revolve wagon	16 x 16 metres
Diameter of the revolve	15 metres
Maximum distributed load on the revolve	Local loads up to 7.5 kN/m² or 3,000 kg on a 200 x 200 mm area (except within 300 mm of the periphery)
Maximum speed of revolve	1 metre/second at the periphery
Stage wagons operated by the stage wagon controls in the vicinity of each move	
Revolve operated as part of the stage control system	

STAGE EQUALISER AND COMPENSATOR ELEVATORS	
Number of equaliser elevators	25 full size and one half size (adjacent to cloth store elevator)
Plan size of each equaliser elevator	4 metres (upstage) x 16 metres (across stage)
Travel	300 mm
Static loading raised or lowered	7.5 kN/m² up to maximum including local loads of 3,000 kg on 200 x 200 mm area
Dynamic loading (nominal)	4,000 kg (do not raise or lower wagons or scenery)
Number of compensator elevators	4 (2 adjacent to the mainstage and 2 adjacent to the rear stage)
Plan size of each compensator elevator	16 metres (upstage) x 8 metres (across stage)
Travel	300 mm
Static loading	7.5 kN/m² including 3,000 kg on 200 x 200 mm area
Dynamic loading (nominal)	6,000 kg (do not raise or lower wagons or scenery)
Stage equaliser and compensator elevators are operated locally by the stage wagon controls	

ORCHESTRA PIT ELEVATORS	
Number of elevators	One double-deck elevator adjacent to the stage front and two single-deck elevators in the auditorium
Travel of double deck elevator	8 metres
Travel of single deck elevators	1.5 metres
Maximum speed of double deck elevator	9 metres /minute
Speed of single deck elevators	2.2 metres /minute
Maximum dynamic payload of elevators	10,000kg each
Maximum static load	5 kN/m^2
Area of orchestra pit under overhang	28 m^2
Approximate area of opera orchestra pit	121 m^2 including overhang
Approximate area of large orchestra pit	140 m^2 including overhang
Orchestra pit elevators are operated using its own control station which allows elevators to be operated in synchronisation	
The seating wagons are plugged into power sockets and the blowers operated with a deadman's handle control enabling the wagons to be pushed around by hand	

MUSICAL INSTRUMENT ELEVATOR	
Travel of elevator	12.5 metres
Speed of elevator	18 metres /minute
Maximum dynamic load	5,000kg
Maximum static load	5 kN/m^2
The musical instrument elevator is adjacent to the orchestra pit and travels from this level down to the orchestra rehearsal room below the auditorium	

SCENERY LIFT	
Size of elevator	11m x 3.5 m x 3.6m high
Travel of elevator	13.2 metres
Speed of elevator	150mm /second 9 metres /minute
Maximum dynamic load	15,000kg
Maximum static load	7.5 kN/m^2
The scenery lift is located upstage of the rear stage and travels from this level down to the repertoire store under the rear stage and up to the scene dock of the studio stage	

Stage Lighting Equipment
Initial purchase schedule showing options

EQUIPMENT FOR MAIN STAGE	
AUDITORIUM Lighting positions	
Source Four 19/26 profile	10
ADB Warp or Robert Juliat Zoom profile 15-30°	24
1.2 kW Robert Juliat or ADB Zoom profile 11-26°	30
2.5 kW Robert Juliat or ADB Zoom profile 10-25°	60
ETC Revolution or ADB Motorised Warp	12
Quasar Silent Flash or Martin Atomic 3000	4
PROSCENIUM Architectural proscenium	
Source Four 19/26 profile	18
Halospot-Rampe Limax HSR 40/2-2R	2
STAGE FRONT Footlights	
Footlights 2/4 colour	10
PORTAL Lower bridge - Lower Rail	
2.5 kW Strand or ADB Studio Fresnel	6
Source Four 19/26 profile	8
HES StudioColor CMY	7
Limax HFR 250/4 or 300w Coda 4	20
Quasar Silent Flash or Martin Atomic 3000	3
PORTAL Lower bridge - Upper Rail	
1.2 kW Robert Juliat or ADB Europe Zoom profile 11-26°	20
PORTAL Top Bridge	
1.2 kW Robert Juliat or ADB Europe Zoom profile 11-26°	12
2.5 kW Robert Juliat or ADB Zoom profile 10-25°	6
PORTAL TOWER Perch Left	
1.2 kW Robert Juliat or ADB Europe Zoom profile 16-35°	12
2.5 kW ADB or Strand Studio PC	4
2.5 kW HMI Robert Juliat Heloise follow spot including stand	1

PORTAL TOWER Perch Right	
1.2 kW Robert Juliat or ADB Europe Zoom profile 16-35°	12
2.5 kW ADB or Strand Studio Pc	4
2.5 kW HMI Robert Juliat Heloise follow spot including stand	1
OVERSTAGE Electric 2	
2.5 kW Strand or ADB Studio Fresnel	15
4 kW HMI Fresnel on L/T yoke, moto barndoor, shutter and scroller	2
HES StudioColor CMY	7
2.5 kW PC on L/T yoke and scroller	2
Limax HFR 250/4 or 300w Coda 4	20
Scroller 15"	5
Quasar Silent Flash or Martin Atomic 3000	2
PSU LT	2
PSU Scroller	1

OVERSTAGE Electric 3	
2.5 kW Strand or ADB Studio Fresnel	15
4 kW HMI Fresnel on L/T yoke, moto barndoor, shutter and scroller	1
HES StudioColor CMY	6
2.5 kW PC on L/T yoke and scroller	2
Limax HFR 250/4 or 300w Coda 4	20
Scroller 15"	5
Quasar Silent Flash or Martin Atomic 3000	2
PSU LT	2
PSU Scroller	1

OVERSTAGE Electric 4	
2.5 kW Strand or ADB Studio Fresnel	15
4 kW HMI Fresnel on L/T yoke, moto barndoor, shutter and scroller	2
HES StudioColor CMY	7
2.5 kW PC on L/T yoke and scroller	2
Limax HFR 250/4 or 300w Coda 4	20
Scroller 15"	5
Quasar Silent Flash or Martin Atomic 3000	2
PSU LT	2
PSU Scroller	1

OVERSTAGE Electric 5	
2.5 kW Strand or ADB Studio Fresnel	15
4 kW HMI Fresnel on L/T yoke, moto barndoor, shutter and scroller	1
HES StudioColor CMY	6
2.5 kW PC on L/T Yoke and scroller	2
Limax HFR 250/4 or 300w Coda 4	20
Scroller 15"	5
Quasar Silent Flash or Martin Atomic 3000	2
PSU LT	2
PSU Scroller	1

OVERSTAGE Electric 6	
2.5 kW Strand or ADB Studio Fresnel	15
4 kW HMI Fresnel on L/T yoke, moto barndoor, shutter and scroller	2
ARRI Sun 4 kW HMI on L/T yoke and shutter	2

HES StudioColor CMY	7
Limax HFR 250/4 or 300w Coda 4	20
Scroller 15"	5
1250 W Flood ADB or CCT	27
1250 W Flood ADB or CCT plus scroller	9
Quasar Silent Flash or Martin Atomic 3000	2
PSU LT	2
PSU Scroller	1
OVERSTAGE BACKLIGHT Electric 7	
1250 W Flood ADB or CCT	18
1250 W Flood ADB or CCT plus scroller	18
5000 W Flood Limax	12
FIRST GALLERY Left	
1.2 kW Robert Juliat or ADB Zoom profile 11-26°	20
2.5 kW Robert Juliat or ADB Zoom profile 10-25°	10
2.5 kW HMI Robert Juliat Zoom profile 9-26°	4
Quasar Silent Flash or Martin Atomic 3000	2
FIRST GALLERY Right	
1.2 kW Robert Juliat or ADB Zoom profile 15-30°	20
2,5 kW Robert Juliat or ADB Zoom profile 10-25°	10
2,5 kW HMI Robert Juliat Zoom profile 9-26°	4
Quasar Silent Flash or Martin Atomic 3000	2
LIGHTING GALLERY Left	
1.2 kW Robert Juliat or ADB Zoom profile 11-26°	20
Quasar Silent Flash or Martin Atomic 3000	2
LIGHTING GALLERY Right	
1.2 kW Robert Juliat or ADB Zoom profile 11-26°	20
Quasar Silent Flash or Martin Atomic 3000	2
ON STAGE LIGHTING BOOMS (10 No)	
1.2 kW Robert Juliat Zoom profile	100
Stage Lighting Booms	10

CYCLORAMA Lighting	
Cyclormama 5000 W Flood Limax	30
EQUIPMENT FOR GENERAL USE	
Source Four 19/26 profile	20
1.2 kW Robert Juliat or ADB Zoom profile 11-26°	10
2.5 kW Robert Juliat or ADB Zoom profile 10-25°	10
2 kW Standard Fresnel ADB or Strand	10
5 kW Tungsten Fresnel ADB or Strand	6
2.5 kW HMI DMX 512 Remote control conventional ballast	2
4 kW HMI DMX 512 Remote control conventional ballast	2
DHA Lightcurtain	8
Cyclormama ground row 1,2 kW 4 cell	18
Scroller 8"	20
Scroller 6"	20
PSU Scroller	6
Quasar Silent Flash or Martin Atomic 3000	2
FOLLOW SPOTS	
2500 HMI Robert Juliat Cyrano follow spot	4
Follow spot stands	4

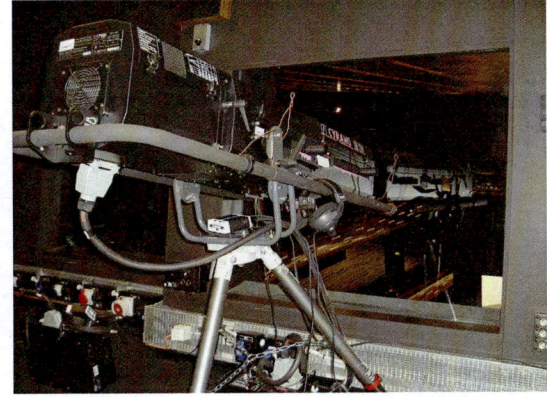

CABLE AND ACCESSORIES	
Extension Cable 1m	150
Extension Cable 2m	150
Extension Cable 3m	100
Extension Cable 5m	100
Extension Cable 10m	100
Extension Cable 20m	50
Submarines CEE split	50
DMX Cable 1m	30
DMX Cable 5m	40
DMX Cable 10m	30
Standard clamps and hooks	550
Quick trigger clamp	200
TV Quick trigger clamp	75
Iris Source Four	30
Iris Zoom profile	30
Gel Frame Cyc 3 shows	180
Boom arms, stands and accessories for use in tower, portal and FOH	LOT

EQUIPMENT FOR STUDIO STAGE	
Source Four 19 profile	20
Source Four 26 profile	30
1.2 kW R&J Zoom profile	30
1.2 kW Standard Fresnel	20
2 kW Standard Fresnel	20
2.5 kW HMI	3
Parcans	20
Stands	10
Standard clamps and hooks	150
Quick trigger clamp	50
Extension Cable 1m	30
Extension Cable 2m	30
Extension Cable 5m	50
Extension Cable 10m	30
Extension Cable 20m	20
Submarines CEE split	40
DMX Cable 1m	20

Main Auditorium Sound Equipment Schedules

Initial purchase list as compiled by the Royal Theatre.
(Note that changes were made during the acquisition process as mentioned in the text)

FRONT-OF-HOUSE - PA Main Stage (L-Acoustics)	
112 XT, high power coax 12"/1,4"	8
ETR 112XT Ophæng	8
LA 24, 2 x 1100W Amplifiers	8
CENTRE SYSTEM (L-Acoustics)	
ARCS 2-way active 15" / 1,4"	5
ARCOUPL x 2 H-Bracket for 2 ARCS	10
BUMP3 moveable	2
LIFTBAR	1
LA 24a 2 x 1100W Amplifiers	3
SUBWOOFER System (L-Acoustics)	
SB118, 1 x 18"	4
LA24a 2 x 1100W Amplifiers	2
FRONT FILL (L-Acoustics)	
MTD108A, 2-Way COAX 8"/ 1"	6
ETR8, Bracket for 1 x 108A	6
LA15a, 4 x 370W	2
UNDER BALCONY Delay (Renkus Heinz)	
TRC51 - Black Full Range System	84
BRCKTU/51Black, "SPECIAL" U-bracket	84
LA15a, 4 x 370W	6
FRONT OF 4 BALCONY Delay (L-Acoustics)	
MTD108A, 2-Way COAX 8"/ 1"	8
ETR8, Bracket for 1 x 108A	8
LA15a, 4 x 370W	1

FRONT OF 1 BALCONY Surround (L-Acoustics)	
MTD108A, 2-Way COAX 8"/ 1"	10
ETR8, Bracket for 1 x 108A	10
LA15a, 4 x 370W.	2

SPEAKER CONTROL SYSTEM (BSS SoundWeb)	
PA / Delay	
SoundWeb 9088ii, 8in- 8out	4
SoundWeb 9088, 8out	4
SoundWeb 9010 Programmable Remote	1

STAGE MONITORS (L-Acoustics)	
115XT high power Coax 15"/1,4"	9
ETR115XT, Bracket	9
LA17a, 2 x 430W.	9

STAGE MONITORS 100V (TOA)	
F-160WP two way BASS-Reflex 51/4" cone / 1" dome tweeter	10
YS-150WP (Black) bracket	10
Stands for speakers	8

MONITORS / SELF-POWERED SPEAKERS (AXYS)	
Axys U-12+	10
Axys U-14	10
Stands for speakers	10

SELF-POWERED SPEAKERS (Fostex)	
6301X (XLR)	10

SELF-POWERED SPEAKERS (Meyer)	
CQ1 (Main Stage Monitor)	4

SOUND MIXERS (Yamaha)	
PM1D Auditorium	1
Remote PM1D (Teqsas) RECO	1

01V96 Audiomix for Video	1
Midi Controller PM1D	1
PRE-AMP (Universal Audio)	
Mic. Pre Amp. Mod. 6176	2
MICRO PORTS including Status Monitoring	
Receiver EM 3532-U	6
Transmitter SK 50 A	12
Batt pack B-50-1	12
Transmitter SKM 5000 UHF-N-BK	4
Batt pack BK 5000-1	4
Mic head Neumann KK 105 S	4
Transmitter SKP 30-U	4
Antenna Booster AB 1036 UHF	2
Ground plane GZA 1036-TV	2
Activ Antenna Splitter ASX 209	1
Receiver EK 3041-U	1
Stand alone GA 3041-C	1
Batt adaptor GA 3041-B	1
Batt pack B 250-1	1
Adapter to EK GA 3041-15	1
Remote software S-MCD 3000-HP	1
Data cable link KX 3500	5
Data cable from CPU to EM 3532-U	1
Lap-top for monitoring MP overview	1
PCMCIA cart 77936	1
TELEVISION CAMERA EQUIPMENT	
Camera (Smaler) SONY DSR-PD170P	1
Camera (Handy) DSR-TRV80E	1
Camera Sony DXC-D50P	1
Camera Sony DXC-D50PX	1
Camera viewer Sony DXF-51	1
Fujiron Focus Remote FSD11	2
Fujiron Focus Remote , MOTOR FSM30	2

Camera CCU Sony CCU-M5AP	1
CCU cable Sony CCZ-A25	1
Camera stand SACHTLER	1
Camera robot CAMS MD	1
TV Monitor Sony PVM 14L3	1
DV record/play Sony DSR45P	1
DVD PLAY / RECORD / EDIT	
DVD recorder SONY RDR-GX7	1
DVD player (AUDIO) SONY DVP-F41MS	1
DVD player SONY DVP-NS930	1
DVD player Pioneer DVD-V7300D	2
Software VEGAS+DVD architect	1
Software SAWStudio(Full)	1
Software NERO burn	1
Computer (as specified)	1
Sound cart Lynx2 Audio	1
Hard disk external Maxtor 200GB, 7200rpm	2
PLAYBACK EQUIPMENT	
MC record/play Denon DN-M991RM	2
CD player Denon DN-C635	2
DAT record/play Sony PCMR500	1
Computer (as specified)	1
Sound cart ECHO layla 24 bit	1
Converter for SFX Steinberg NUENDO DD8	1
Software SFX proAudio show control	1
Software VEGAS+DVD architect	1
Software SAW Studio (Full)	1
Software Sequoia	1
Software Cool Edite	1
Software NERO burn	1
Headphones Sony MDR-V700DJ	4
VIDEO PLAYBACK EQUIPMENT	
DVD player Pioneer DVD-V7300D	2

Software VEGAS+DVD architect	1
Software SAW Studio (Full)	1
Software NERO burn	1
Software Mediator 7 Pro	1
Computer (as specified)	1
Sound cart Lynx2 Audio	1
Video mixer FOCUS MXProDV	1
Video Monitor Sony LMD 530 3x5.6"	1
Hard disk external Maxtor 200GB, 7200rpm	1
Computer for remote Sony Vario laptop	1
DV CAMERA RECORD / PLAY	
DV record/play Sony DSR45P	1
DV record/play Sony DSR 11	1
Video Monitor Sony PVM 14L	1
AUDITORIUM CONTROL ROOM MONITOR	
1030AM (Pair) Desk (Genelec)	1
1029A (Pair) Video Rec. (Genelec)	1
WALKIE-TALKIE (Motorolla / ZENITEL)	
Wireless Radio GP344	4
Headset for GP 344	4
Battery Charger for GP 344	4
Programming for GP 344	4
JACKFIELD	
B-Gauge Jackfield 45-220 Moses & Mitchell	3
DK-AUDIO Facemeter	
Master Stereo Display MSD 600M /SA 3 x in / 1 x out	2

Studio Stage Sound Equipment Schedules
Initial purchase list as compiled by the Royal Theatre.
(Note that changes were made during the acquisition process)

FRONT OF HOUSE - Left and Right (L-Acoustics)	
112 XT, high power coax 12"/1,4"	6
ETR 112XT Ophæng	6
LA 24, 2 x 1100W. AMP.	6
Centre System (L-Acoustics)	
115XT high power Coax 15"/1,4"	3
ETR115XT, Bracket	3
LA17a, 2 x 430W.	3
SUBWOOFER System (L-Acoustics)	
SB118, 1 x 18"	2
LA24a 2x 1100W.	1
FRONT FILL (L-Acoustics)	
MTD108A, 2-Way COAX 8"/ 1"	6
ETR8, Bracket for 1 x 108A	6
LA15a, 4 x 370W.	2
Speaker Control System (BSS SoundWeb)	
PA / Delay	
SoundWeb 9088ii, 8 in - 8 out	2
SoundWeb 9088, 8 out	2
STAGE MONITORS (L-Acoustics)	
115XT high power Coax 15"/1,4"	6
ETR115XT, Bracket	6
LA17a, 2 x 430W.	6
STAGE MONITORS, 100V. (TOA)	
F-160WP, TWO WAY BASS-Reflex 51/4" cone / 1" dome tweeter	4
YS-150WP (Black) Bracket	4
Stands for speakers	4

MONITORS / SELF POWERED SPEAKERS (AXYS)	
Axys U-12+	2
Axys U-14	2
Stands for speakers	2

SOUND MIXERS (Yamaha)	
DM2000, Studie Scenen	1
01V96 Audiomix for Video	1
Master Stereo Display DK-Audio MSD 600M /SA 3xin/1xout	1

PRE AMPLIFIER (Universal Audio)	
Mic. Pre Amp. Mod. 6176	1

MICRO PORTS including Status Monitoring	
Receiver EM 3532-U	3
Transmitter SK 50 A	6
Batt pack B-50-1	6
Mic head Neumann KK 105 S	2
Transmitter SKP 30-U	2
Antenna Booster AB 1036 UHF	2
Ground plane GZA 1036-TV	2
Active Antenna Splitter ASX 209	1
Remote software S-MCD 3000-HP	1
Data cable link KX 3500	5
Data cable from CPU to EM 3532-U	1
Lap Top for monitoring MP overview	1
PCMCIA cart 77936	1

DV CAMERA RECORD / PLAY	
DV record/play Sony DSR45P	1
DVD recorder SONY RDR-GX7	1
Video Monitor Sony PVM 14L3	1
Camera SONY	1
Camera stand	1

PLAYBACK EQUIPMENT	
MC record/play Denon DN-M991RM	2

CD player Denon DN-C635	2
DVD player Pioneer DVD-V7300D	2
DV record/play Sony DSR45P	1
Computer (as specification)	1
Sound cart ECHO layla 24 bit	1
Converter for SFX Steinberg NUENDO DD8	1
Video mixer FOCUS MXProDV	1
Software SFX proAudio show control	1
Software VEGAS+DVD architect	1
Software Sequoia	1
Software SAW Studio (Full)	1
Software Cool Edite	1
Software Mediator 7 Pro	1
Software NERO burn	1
Video Monitor Sony LMD 530 3x5.6"	1
Headphones Sony MDR-V700DJ	2
Computer for remote Sony Vario laptop	1

Note that similar equipment was purchased for use in the Rehearsal Stage, Rehearsal Rooms, the Audio-Visual Suite, Video Copying Room and Main Patch Room. Minor items such as racks and trolleys, splitter boxes, cables and accessories are not shown.

Stage Lighting Equipment 2
Final schedule as purchased

	No
AUDITORIUM	
ETC Source Four 19/26 profile	10
1.2 kW Robert Juliat Zoom profile 16-35°	22
1.2 kW Robert Juliat Zoom profile 11-26°	24
2.5 kW Robert Juliat Zoom profile 10-25°	12
2.5 kW Robert Juliat Zoom profile 9-16°	44
ETC Revolution	6
Quasar Silent Flash	4
ARCHITECTURAL PROSCENIUM	
ETC Source Four 19/26 profile	14
PORTAL Lower Bridge - Lower Rail	
2.5 kW DeSisti Studio Fresnel pole operated	6
HES StudioColor CMY	6
Quasar Silent Flash	2
PORTAL Lower Bridge - Upper Rail	
1.2 kW Robert Juliat Zoom profile 11-26°	14
PORTAL Top Bridge - Lower Rail	
Limax HFA 500/4	18
1.2 kW Robert Juliat Zoom profile 11-26°	12
PORTAL Top Bridge	
1.2 kW Robert Juliat Zoom profile 11-26°	12
PORTAL TOWER Perch Left	
1.2 kW Robert Juliat Zoom profile 16-35°	12
2.5 kW DeSisti Studio Fresnel	1

PORTAL TOWER Perch Right	
1.2 kW Robert Juliat Zoom profile 16-35°	12
2.5 kW DeSisti Studio Fresnel	1
OVERSTAGE Electric 1	
2.5 kW DeSisti Studio Fresnel Pole operated	15
Licht-technik Yoke incl. Stargate, Mag Vader and 4kW ARRI HMI Fresnel theatre version complete with electronic ballast	2
HES StudioColor CMY	6
Licht-technik Yoke incl. Stargate, Mag Max mk2 and 5kW Fresnel theatre version complete	2
Limax HFA 500/4	18
Rainbow scroller 15"	5
Quasar Silent Flash	2
PSU LT	2
PSU Scroller	1
Vari*Lite 3500	3
OVERSTAGE Electric 2	
2.5 kW DeSisti Studio Fresnel pole operated	15
Licht-technik Yoke incl. Stargate, Mag Vader and 4kW ARRI HMI Fresnel theatre version complete with electronic ballast	1
HES StudioColor CMY	6
Licht-technik Yoke incl. Stargate, Mag Max mk2 and 5kW Fresnel theatre version complete	2
Limax HFA 500/4	18
Rainbow scroller 15"	5
Quasar Silent Flash	2
PSU LT	2
PSU Scroller	1
Vari*Lite 3500	4
OVERSTAGE Electric 3	
2.5 kW DeSisti Studio Fresnel pole operated	15
Licht-technik Yoke incl. Stargate, Mag Vader and 4kW ARRI HMI Fresnel theatre version complete with electronic ballast	2

HES StudioColor CMY	6
Licht-technik Yoke incl. Stargate, Mag Max mk2 and 5kW Fresnel theatre version complete	2
Limax HFA 500/4	18
Rainbow scroller 15"	5
Quasar Silent Flash	2
PSU LT	2
PSU Scroller	1
Vari*Lite 3500	3
OVERSTAGE Electric 4	
2.5 kW DeSisti Studio Fresnel pole operated	15
Licht-technik Yoke incl. Stargate, Mag Vader and 4kW ARRI HMI Fresnel theatre version complete with electronic ballast	1
HES StudioColor CMY	6
Licht-technik Yoke incl. Stargate, Mag Max mk2 and 5kW Fresnel theatre version complete	2
Limax HFA 500/4	18
Rainbow scroller 15"	5
Quasar Silent Flash	2
PSU LT	3
PSU Scroller	1
Vari*Lite 3500	1
OVERSTAGE Electric 5	
2.5 kW DeSisti Studio Fresnel pole operated	15
Licht-technik Yoke incl. Mag Vader and 4kW ArriSun HMI complete with. electronic ballast	2
HES StudioColor CMY	6
Limax HFA 500/4	18
Rainbow scroller 15"	5
Limax HFA 2000 Flood + 2 set of gel frames	36
Limax 5000 W Flood incl. Licht-Technik XXL scroller	6
Quasar Silent Flash	2
PSU LT	3

PSU Scroller	1
Vari*Lite 3500	1
OVERSTAGE BACKLIGHT Electric 6	
Limax HFA 2000 Flood + 2 set of gel frames	36
Limax 5000 W Flood incl. Licht-Technik XXL scroller	12
1st. GALLERY Left	
1.2 kW Robert Juliat Zoom profile 11-26°	20
2.5 kW Robert Juliat Zoom profile 10-25°	10
2.5 kW HMI Robert Juliat Zoom profile 9-26°	4
Quasar Silent Flash	2
1st. GALLERY Right	
1.2 kW Robert Juliat Zoom profile 11-26°	20
2.5 kW Robert Juliat Zoom profile 10-25°	10
2.5 kW HMI Robert Juliat Zoom profile 9-26°	4
Quasar Silent Flash	2
LIGHTING GALLERY Left	
1.2 kW Robert Juliat Zoom profile 11-26°	20
Quasar Silent Flash	2
LIGHTING GALLERY Right	
1.2 kW Robert Juliat Zoom profile 11-26°	20
Quasar Silent Flash	2
ON STAGE LIGHTING BOOMS (10 No)	
1.2 kW Robert Juliat Zoom profile 16-35°	40
1.2 kW Robert Juliat Zoom profile 11-26°	60
2.5 kW Robert Juliat PC incl. 12" Rainbow scroller	20
CYCLORAMA	
Limax Cyclormama 5000 W	30

EQUIPMENT FOR CENTRAL USE	
5 kW Tungsten Fresnel Strand	6
2.5 kW HMI Dmx 512 Remote control conventional ballast	2
4 kW HMI Dmx 512 Remote control conventional ballast	2
DHA Lightcurtain with pitching	8
Cyclormama ground row 1.2 kW 4 cell + 2 set of gel frames	20
Rainbow scroller 8"	12
Rainbow scroller 6"	12
PSU Scroller	8
Quasar Silent Flash	2
E\T\C Pigi 700S, 4kW projector	4
FOLLOWSPOTS	
2500 HMI Robert Juliat Cyrano followspot	4

17 AN IMPRESSION OF OPERAEN
Tobi Tobias

If, from the entrance of the Old Stage, you walk down the picturesque canal street of Nyhavn, you'll see the imposing Opera across the water, on the island of Holmen. You get to it by boat. The ride across the water takes exactly three minutes, and the boat is merely a small ferry, but still…

The building itself, with its curvilinear shape and an overhanging roof that seems to float, makes you think "ship." This is only appropriate, since the formidably costly structure was the gift of a man, one A.P. Møller, whose family made its fortune in ship building and transporting cargo over the water.

The Opera is masterly in its command of space and light and typically Danish in its harmonious juxtaposition of materials: glass (miles of it, it would seem), stone (in subdued shades of grey and sand that give it an eerie lightness), steely metal, and lovingly treated wood. The interior of the building continually echoes the curved shape of the façade. At the hub of the public space is a gigantic bowed form clad in glowing maple veneer. Fantasy suggests it's the work of a violin maker operating on a Brobdingnagian scale. Exquisitely varied in its grain, burnished to a rich copper sheen, the wood looks as if each piece had been chosen for its singular beauty and placed so as to make a spectrum of subtle contrasts with its neighbouring pieces. The convex side of this structure is the spatial and decorative heart of the building's tiered promenades. Functionally – as if it were there merely to be useful – it forms the outer shell of the auditorium. Discovering its double life is a small but very particular delight.

At every level of the promenades – there are four of them over the ground floor – you can look out over the water, through the horizon-wide curved windows, setting your drink, libretto, or glittering *minaudière* on the narrow steel shelf placed at ship's-rail height, and pretend you are on a pleasure cruise, sailing for the destiny of your dreams. You can dine on the promenades too; one malcontent observed that the Opera was conceived as a bar/restaurant with entertainment. The audience likes it, though, and dresses up marvellously to be players in the scene – the elder and wealthier in an expensively tasteful mode Scandinavian fashion has brought to a high and perfect pitch, the young with unquenchable rakish imagination.

Like the best Danish design for the home, particularly the sublime "Danish Modern" furniture of the mid-twentieth century, the Opera manages to be both austere and welcoming. Its sole concession to a lower-brow yen for glitter rests in a trio of round chandeliers – more than ten feet in diameter, I'd guess – that are suspended over the first tier. Faceted like supersized Swaroski crystals, the globes gaudily refract tones of silver, cool gold, rose, and ultramarine. A grid inside them is studded with tiny lights on stems – for all the world like a giant's matchsticks.

From the promenades, gangways lead to the auditorium's seating areas, adding to the visitor's general impression of being on a luxury ship, safely ensconced in elegance, with a view of the world outside that he or she is blithely gliding past. The most splendid view of that world is to be had at the two highest tiers. That perspective best reveals the small ornate towers of Old Copenhagen, springing up from the otherwise modestly low cityscape, as if they were cunningly fashioned pop-up toys.

After revelling in the extravagant light and space of the public areas, you're shocked by the enclosed darkness of the auditorium. The contrast constitutes a theatrical coup in itself. The interior is panelled with a Japanese-style arrangement of slatted wood in two tones of brown – deep and deeper. The wood is pierced with little lights so that, once seated, you can actually read your program, but the room as a whole, with its balconies seeming to embrace the stage as you look towards it, instills a feeling of intimacy. In this it declares its cousinship with the Royal Theatre's Old Stage.

Turning your back to the stage and casting your glance upward, however, you see the auditorium's second coup de théâtre. The depth of the four curved balconies creates a sense of immense sweep. This impression of vastness is augmented by the overarching vault of the ceiling (clad like the walls in striated wood). Everywhere the dark wood is pierced with tiny dots and fine lines of light, suggesting the elements that sparkle from an immense distance in a night-time sky. The whole creates an effect of galactic grandeur.

At intermission you can stroll the long swath of a curving outdoor promenade and in the summer watch the sun go down. The last fiery rays drop below the horizon, yet the sky remains luminous and the water graciously reflects it. This coup de théâtre by Mother Nature, co-opted by the Opera's architect, Henning Larsen, makes you feel the universe is holding its breath.

Tobi Tobias lives in New York City, where she writes about dance and other things worth looking at.

She thinks she's best known, nationally and internationally, for her writing about dance. Much of this work appeared in Dance magazine (where she also edited the criticism for nearly a decade) and in New York magazine (where she served as the journal's dance critic for 22 years). Currently, she is the New York-based dance critic for Bloomberg News and contributes frequent feature stories to the Arts & Leisure section of the New York Times.

Her involvement with dance has extended to major oral history projects as well as to writing for the public television series Dance in America and Live from Lincoln Center. In 1992, she was awarded a Danish knighthood in recognition of her extensive writing and oral history project on the Royal Danish Ballet and its Bournonville tradition.

Copenhagen Opera House

ENTERTAINMENT TECHNOLOGY PRESS

FREE SUBSCRIPTION SERVICE

Keeping Up To Date with

Copenhagen Opera House

Entertainment Technology titles are continually up-dated, and all major changes and additions are listed in date order in the relevant dedicated area of the publisher's website. Simply go to the front page of www.etnow.com and click on the BOOKS button. From there you can locate the title and be connected through to the latest information and services related to the publication.

The author of the title welcomes comments and suggestions about the book and can be contacted by email at:
editor@etnow.com

Titles Published by Entertainment Technology Press

ABC of Theatre Jargon *Francis Reid* **£9.95** ISBN 1904031099
This glossary of theatrical terminology explains the common words and phrases that are used in normal conversation between actors, directors, designers, technicians and managers.

Aluminium Structures in the Entertainment Industry *Peter Hind* **£24.95** ISBN 1904031064
Aluminium Structures in the Entertainment Industry aims to educate the reader in all aspects of the design and safe usage of temporary and permanent aluminium structures specific to the entertainment industry – such as roof structures, PA towers, temporary staging, etc.

AutoCAD – A Handbook for Theatre Users *David Ripley* **£24.95** ISBN 1904031315
From 'Setting Up' to 'Drawing in Three Dimensions' via 'Drawings Within Drawings', this compact and fully illustrated guide to AutoCAD covers everything from the basics to full colour rendering and remote plotting.

Basics – A Beginner's Guide to Lighting Design *Peter Coleman* **£9.95** ISBN 1904031412
The fourth in the author's 'Basics' series, this title covers the subject area in four main sections: The Concept, Practical Matters, Related Issues and The Design Into Practice. In an area that is difficult to be definitive, there are several things that cross all the boundaries of all lighting design and it's these areas that the author seeks to help with.

Basics – A Beginner's Guide to Special Effects *Peter Coleman* **£9.95** ISBN 1904031331
This title introduces newcomers to the world of special effects. It describes all types of special effects including pyrotechnic, smoke and lighting effects, projections, noise machines, etc. It places emphasis on the safe storage, handling and use of pyrotechnics.

Basics – A Beginner's Guide to Stage Lighting *Peter Coleman* **£9.95** ISBN 190403120X
This title does what it says: it introduces newcomers to the world of stage lighting. It will not teach the reader the art of lighting design, but will teach beginners much about the 'nuts and bolts' of stage lighting.

Basics – A Beginner's Guide to Stage Sound *Peter Coleman* **£9.95** ISBN 1904031277
This title does what it says: it introduces newcomers to the world of stage sound. It will not teach the reader the art of sound design, but will teach beginners much about the background to sound reproduction in a theatrical environment.

Building Better Theaters *Michael Mell* **£16.95** 1904031404
A title within our Consultancy Series, this book describes the process of designing a theater, from the initial decision to build through to opening night. Mr. Mell's book provides a step-by-step guide to the design and construction of performing arts facilities. Chapters discuss: assembling your team, selecting an architect, different construction methods, the architectural design process, construction of the theater, theatrical systems and equipment, the stage, backstage, the auditorium, ADA requirements and the lobby. Each chapter clearly describes what to expect and how to avoid surprises. It is a must-read for architects, planners, performing arts groups, educators and anyone who may be considering building or renovating a theater.

A Comparative Study of Crowd Behaviour at Two Major Music Events
Chris Kemp, Iain Hill, Mick Upton **£7.95** ISBN 1904031250
A compilation of the findings of reports made at two major live music concerts, and in particular crowd behaviour, which is followed from ingress to egress.

Copenhagen Opera House *Richard Brett and John Offord* **£32.00** ISBN 1904031420
Completed in a little over three years, the Copenhagen Opera House opened with a royal gala performance on 15th January 2005. Built on a spacious brown-field site, the building is a landmark venue and this book provides the complete technical background story to an opera house set to become a benchmark for future design and planning. Sixteen chapters by relevant experts involved with the project cover everything from the planning of the auditorium and studio stage, the stage engineering, stage lighting and control and architectural lighting through to acoustic design and sound technology plus technical summaries.

Electrical Safety for Live Events *Marco van Beek* **£16.95** ISBN 1904031285
This title covers electrical safety regulations and good pracitise pertinent to the entertainment industries and includes some basic electrical theory as well as clarifying the "do's and don't's" of working with electricity.

The Exeter Theatre Fire *David Anderson* **£24.95** ISBN 1904031137
This title is a fascinating insight into the events that led up to the disaster at the Theatre Royal, Exeter, on the night of September 5th 1887. The book details what went wrong, and the lessons that were learned from the event.

Fading Light – A Year in Retirement *Francis Reid* **£14.95** ISBN 1904031358
Francis Reid, the lighting industry's favourite author, describes a full year in retirement. "Old age is much more fun than I expected," he says. Fading Light describes visits and experiences to the author's favourite theatres and opera houses, places of relaxation and re-visits to scholarly intitutions.

Focus on Lighting Technology *Richard Cadena* **£17.95** ISBN 1904031145
This concise work unravels the mechanics behind modern performance lighting and appeals to designers and technicians alike. Packed with clear, easy-to-read diagrams, the book provides excellent explanations behind the technology of performance lighting.

Health and Safety Aspects in the Live Music Industry *Chris Kemp, Iain Hill* **£30.00** ISBN 1904031226
This title includes chapters on various safety aspects of live event production and is written by specialists in their particular areas of expertise.

Health and Safety Management in the Live Music and Events Industry *Chris Hannam* **£25.95** ISBN 1904031307
This title covers the health and safety regulations and their application regarding all aspects of staging live entertainment events, and is an invaluable manual for production managers and event organisers.

Hearing the Light – 50 Years Backstage *Francis Reid* **£24.95** ISBN 1904031188
This highly enjoyable memoir delves deeply into the theatricality of the industry. The author's almost fanatical interest in opera, his formative period as lighting designer at Glyndebourne and his experiences as a theatre administrator, writer and teacher make for a broad and unique background.

An Introduction to Rigging in the Entertainment Industry *Chris Higgs* **£24.95**
ISBN 1904031129
This book is a practical guide to rigging techniques and practices and also thoroughly covers safety issues and discusses the implications of working within recommended guidelines and regulations.

Let There be Light – Entertainment Lighting Software Pioneers in Interview
Robert Bell **£32.00** ISBN 1904031242
Robert Bell interviews a distinguished group of software engineers working on entertainment lighting ideas and products.

Lighting for Roméo and Juliette *John Offord* **£26.95** ISBN 1904031161
John Offord describes the making of the Vienna State Opera production from the lighting designer's viewpoint – from the point where director Jürgen Flimm made his decision not to use scenery or sets and simply employ the expertise of LD Patrick Woodroffe.

Lighting Systems for TV Studios *Nick Mobsby* **£45.00** ISBN 1904031005
Lighting Systems for TV Studios, now in its second edition, is the first book specifically written on the subject and has become the 'standard' resource work for studio planning and design covering the key elements of system design, luminaires, dimming, control, data networks and suspension systems as well as detailing the infrastructure items such as cyclorama, electrical and ventilation. Sensibly TV lighting principles are explained and some history on TV broadcasting, camera technology and the equipment is provided to help set the scene! The second edition includes applications for sine wave and distributed dimming, moving lights, Ethernet and new cool lamp technology.

Lighting Techniques for Theatre-in-the-Round *Jackie Staines* **£24.95**
ISBN 1904031013
Lighting Techniques for Theatre-in-the-Round is a unique reference source for those working on lighting design for theatre-in-the-round for the first time. It is the first title to be published specifically on the subject, it also provides some anecdotes and ideas for more challenging shows, and attempts to blow away some of the myths surrounding lighting in this format.

Lighting the Stage *Francis Reid* **£14.95** ISBN 1904031080
Lighting the Stage discusses the human relationships involved in lighting design – both between people, and between these people and technology. The book is written from a highly personal viewpoint and its 'thinking aloud' approach is one that Francis Reid has used in his writings over the past 30 years.

Model National Standard Conditions *ABTT/DSA/LGLA* **£20.00** ISBN 1904031110
These *Model National Standard Conditions* covers operational matters and complement *The Technical Standards for Places of Entertainment*, which describes the physical requirements for building and maintaining entertainment premises.

Mr Phipps' Theatre *Mark Jones, John Pick* **£17.95** ISBN: 1904031382
Mark Jones and John Pick describe "The Sensational Story of Eastbourne's Royal Hippodrome" – formerly Eastbourne Theatre Royal. An intriguing narrative, the book sets the story against a unique social history of the town. Peter Longman, former director of The Theatres Trust, provides the Foreword.

Pages From Stages *Anthony Field* **£17.95** ISBN 1904031269
Anthony Field explores the changing style of theatres including interior design, exterior design, ticket and seat prices, and levels of service, while questioning whether the theatre still exists as a place of entertainment for regular theatre-goers.

Practical Dimming *Nick Mobsby* **£22.95** ISBN 19040313447
This important and easy to read title covers the history of electrical and electronic dimming, how dimmers work, current dimmer types from around the world, planning of a dimming system, looking at new sine wave dimming technology and distributed dimming. Integration of dimming into different performance venues as well as the necessary supporting electrical systems are fully detailed. Significant levels of information are provided on the many different forms and costs of potential solutions as well as how to plan specific solutions. Architectural dimming for the likes of hotels, museums and shopping centres are included. Practical Dimming is a companion book to Practical DMX and is designed for all involved in the use, operation and design of dimming systems.

Practical DMX *Nick Mobsby* **£16.95** ISBN 19040313668
In this highly topical and important title the author details the principles of DMX, how to plan a network, how to choose equipment and cables, with data on products from around the world, and how to install DMX networks for shows and on a permanently installed basis. The easy style of the book and the helpful fault finding tips, together with a review of different DMX testing devices provide an ideal companion for all lighting technicians and system designers. An introduction to Ethernet and Canbus networks are provided as well tips on analogue networks and protocol conversion. This title has been recently updated to include a new chapter on Remote Device Management that became an international standard in Summer 2006.

Practical Guide to Health and Safety in the Entertainment Industry
Marco van Beek **£14.95** ISBN 1904031048
This book is designed to provide a practical approach to Health and Safety within the Live Entertainment and Event industry. It gives industry-pertinent examples, and seeks to break down the myths surrounding Health and Safety.

Production Management *Joe Aveline* **£17.95** ISBN 1904031102
Joe Aveline's book is an in-depth guide to the role of the Production Manager, and includes real-life practical examples and 'Aveline's Fables' – anecdotes of his experiences with real messages behind them.

Rigging for Entertainment: Regulations and Practice *Chris Higgs* **£19.95**
ISBN 1904031218
Continuing where he left off with his highly successful *An Introduction to Rigging in the Entertainment Industry*, Chris Higgs' second title covers the regulations and use of equipment in greater detail.

Rock Solid Ethernet *Wayne Howell* **£24.95** ISBN 1904031293
Although aimed specifically at specifiers, installers and users of entertainment industry systems, this book will give the reader a thorough grounding in all aspects of computer networks, whatever industry they may work in. The inclusion of historical and technical 'sidebars' make for an enjoyable as well as informative read.

Sixty Years of Light Work *Fred Bentham* **£26.95** ISBN 1904031072
This title is an autobiography of one of the great names behind the development of modern stage lighting equipment and techniques.

Sound for the Stage *Patrick Finelli* **£24.95** ISBN 1904031153
Patrick Finelli's thorough manual covering all aspects of live and recorded sound for performance is a complete training course for anyone interested in working in the field of stage sound, and is a must for any student of sound.

Stage Lighting Design in Britain: The Emergence of the Lighting Designer, 1881-1950 *Nigel Morgan* **£17.95** ISBN 190403134X
This book sets out to ascertain the main course of events and the controlling factors that determined the emergence of the theatre lighting designer in Britain, starting with the introduction of incandescent electric light to the stage, and ending at the time of the first public lighting design credits around 1950. The book explores the practitioners, equipment, installations and techniques of lighting design.

Stage Lighting for Theatre Designers *Nigel Morgan* **£17.95** ISBN 1904031196
This is an updated second edition of Nigel Morgan's popular book for students of theatre design – outlining all the techniques of stage lighting design.

Technical Marketing Techniques *David Brooks, Andy Collier, Steve Norman* **£24.95** ISBN 190403103X
Technical Marketing is a novel concept, recently defined and elaborated by the authors of this book, with business-to-business companies competing in fast developing technical product sectors.

Technical Standards for Places of Entertainment *ABTT/DSA* **£30.00** ISBN 1904031056
Technical Standards for Places of Entertainment details the necessary physical standards required for entertainment venues.

Theatre Engineering and Stage Machinery *Toshiro Ogawa* **£30.00** ISBN 1904031021
Theatre Engineering and Stage Machinery is a unique reference work covering every aspect of theatrical machinery and stage technology in global terms, and across the complete historical spectrum.

Theatre Lighting in the Age of Gas *Terence Rees* **£24.95** ISBN 190403117X
Entertainment Technology Press has republished this valuable historic work previously produced by the Society for Theatre Research in 1978. *Theatre Lighting in the Age of Gas* investigates the technological and artistic achievements of theatre lighting engineers from the 1700s to the late Victorian period.

Theatre Space: A Rediscovery Reported *Francis Reid* **£19.95** ISBN 1904031439
In the post-war world of the 1950s and 60s, the format of theatre space became a matter for a debate that aroused passions of an intensity unknown before or since. The proscenium arch was clearly identified as the enemy, accused of forming a barrier to disrupt the relations between the actor and audience. An uneasy fellow-traveller at the time, Francis Reid later recorded his impressions whilst enjoying performances or working in theatres old and new and this book is an important collection of his writings in various theatrical journals from 1969-2001 including his contribution to the Cambridge Guide to the Theatre in 1988. It reports some of the flavour of the period when theatre architecture was rediscovering its past in a search to establish its future.

Theatres of Achievement *John Higgins* **£29.95** ISBN: 1904031374
John Higgins affectionately describes the history of 40 distinguished UK theatres in a personal tribute, each uniquely illustrated by the author. Completing each profile is colour photography by Adrian Eggleston.

Walt Disney Concert Hall – The Backstage Story *Patricia MacKay & Richard Pilbrow* **£28.95** ISBN 1904031234
Spanning the 16-year history of the design and construction of the Walt Disney Concert Hall, this book provides a fresh and detailed behind the scenes story of the design and technology from a variety of viewpoints. This is the first book to reveal the "process" of the design of a concert hall.

Yesterday's Lights – A Revolution Reported *Francis Reid* **£26.95** ISBN 1904031323
Set to help new generations to be aware of where the art and science of theatre lighting is coming from – and stimulate a nostalgia trip for those who lived through the period, Francis Reid's latest book has over 350 pages dedicated to the task, covering the 'revolution' from the fifties through to the present day. Although this is a highly personal account of the development of lighting design and technology and he admits that there are 'gaps', you'd be hard put to find anything of significance missing.

Go to www.etbooks.co.uk for full details of above titles and secure online ordering facilities.